"Dr. Elvgren has distilled a lifetime of accrued knowledge, wisdom, and experience into a practical and accessible textbook that will benefit the budding playwright and more accomplished practitioner in equal measure. Elvgren dives into the 'why' behind the writing process for a richer, more purposeful approach. Perhaps more than anything, I am enamored with his organic integration of faith and art. It permeates this text because it is who he is as a theater maker. There is no segregation of the two. He is as much a playwright as he is a Christian and the two cannot simply be bifurcated. This benefits all of us who yearn for a seamless marriage between our faith and art."

—**Bruce Long**, Executive Director, Christians in the Theater Arts

"Dr. Elvgren reminds us that we are wired (created!) for the power of story as image bearing actors. The challenge for those of us who feel called to the theater industry is how to bring God's unfolding story to our broken world without diluting it to dramatic pablum or condescending spin. The Christian playwright, as Gil points out, can confidently tell the truth of God's love with all the frail, sweaty, human vulnerability and Divine mystery one can muster.

—**Scott Nolte**, Founder and Producing Artistic Director Emeritus, Taproot Theater Company

"This book has much to offer for playwrights in all stages of writing development. All aspects of crafting the play, from dialogue to character development, from structure to timing, are covered well. Elvgren's vast knowledge of the theater is evident from the multiple examples he provides from classic and contemporary works. Elvgren's book is much more than a 'how to,' it is a deep and challenging call to create works that will prod the heart and engage the mind. There is a vast and fun intellect behind this book and the reader is in for an adventure."

—**Richard Young**, playwright, producer, professor, and author of *And the Word Became Flesh: Devotionals for Theater Artists*

"Gillette Elvgren's work on playwriting changed the direction of my writing life. The lectures and playwriting exercises he presented in the classroom are also available in this rich and formidable playwriting text. These are pages for the playwright, whatever the level of experience, to garnish in and grow by."

—**Paul D. Patton**, Professor Emeritus of Communication and Theater, Spring Arbor University

# Playwriting

# Playwriting

## A Christian Perspective

GILLETTE ELVGREN

Integratio Press

Pasco, Washington

PLAYWRITING: A CHRISTIAN PERSPECTIVE

This is a publication of Trinity House, a Division of Integratio Press.

Integratio Press is an Imprint of Christianity and Communication Studies Network
11503 Easton Dr.
Pasco, WA 99301

www.theccsn.com

For questions and input into the book, email the author: gillelvjr@gmail.com

Cover design: Carol O'Callaghan
Interior design: Carol O'Callaghan
Image: Depositphotos

PAPERBACK ISBN: 978-1-959685-03-6
EBOOK ISBN: 978-1-959685-04-3

Library of Congress Control Number: 2023943746

# Table of Contents

# Acknowledgments

I WOULD LIKE TO ACKNOWLEDGE AND THANK those artists and mentors that helped to launch me as a writer in the theater domain. Dr. Attilio Favorini, my Chair at the University of Pittsburgh who inspired, supported, and helped to author *Steel/City* (1976). Also, a special bow of the head to Roger Green and Rich Patterson, Children's Sand and Surf Mission (CSSM) leaders, who put up with my early attempts at writing faith-based sketches for kids on the east coast beaches.

Also, a hearty thanks to the artistic directors of the professional theater companies that took the risk of launching original "Elvgren works" in their venues: Ron Reed of Pacific Theater, Vancouver; Jeannette Clift George of A.D. Players, Houston; Robert Smyth of The Lamb's Players, San Diego; Derrick and Jennifer Martin, of Americana Theater Company, Plymouth; Scott Nolte of Taproot Theater Company, Seattle; Nate Fischer, Emerald Coast Theater Company, Florida; and for Regent University in Virginia Beach and Saltworks Theater Company in Pittsburgh for producing my plays as both touring and in-house productions.

Special acknowledgment and thanks go to Carol Jaudes, former *Cats* actress and Salvation Army Arts and Events Director, who premiered three of my one-person shows. I thank Dr. Dale Savidge, former President of Christianity in the Arts, for his friendship and vision, and Bruce Long, professional producer, and Christians in the Theater Arts President, who volunteered to take a red pen to an early draft of this text and whose encouragement and upbeat personality remain a constant comfort.

Editor and publisher Dr. Robert H. Woods Jr. and friend and co-editor Dr. Paul Patton deserve a special acknowledgment for seeing this work through to completion, for their patience, and wise counsel.

Also, to Dr. Buzz McLaughlin, author and friend, for his inspirational book on playwriting, *The Playwright's Process: Learning the Craft from Today's Leading Dramatists* (Back Stage Books, 1997), which I used in graduate classes for years.

Finally, thanks go both to my lovely wife, Betty Jo, who was my first

ACKNOWLEDGMENTS

editor, my helpmate, companion, and support, and to our Lord, our Messiah Jesus, the author of the "creative mandate," through which we are gifted with the ability to tell stories, and through whom all good and right things come into being.

# Introduction

A QUESTION I HAVE ASKED MYSELF OVER TIME IS: why are the faith-based attempts at art, specifically in the theatrical world, seemingly neglected in terms of exposure, debate, and presentation? Part One of this book begins with a tentative exploration of this topical question from both cultural and aesthetic viewpoints. Part Two deals with the various structural components that form the basis for writing an effective drama as well as thematic approaches that include a worldview that does not shy away from "God-cognizance."

The first reason for the shortage of faith-based theatrical offerings is partially due to the difficulty of representing the performing arts in script form. The scripts that serve as their creative source are more equivalent to the intricacies of architectural drawings than the entire embodiment of a work on the written page. They are created and realized through a community of different artistic disciplines oftentimes at great expense. They transform space, time, and action to provide three-dimensional artistic creations that exist fleetingly and then disappear.

The theater exists in the eternal present and can reflect the cultural anomalies that we wake up to every morning. Thus, a rendering of William Shakespeare's *Julius Caesar* (1599) at Playhouse in the Park in New York City in June of 2017 depicts the ancient Roman ruler in the modern likeness of then President Donald Trump.

Perhaps another reason for the "neglect" of the artist of religious persuasion is because his worldview, which is intrinsically linked to his belief system, is considered politically incorrect to the dominant culture's understanding of what should and should not be considered acceptable artistic fare. Where are the plays that can compete in quality and conservative subject matter with the so-called liberal agenda? Or the films? There are works that espouse the Christian faith, but few that brilliantly present a transformative alternative to the dominant culture's dominance over professional theater offerings. *The Observer's* theater critic, Jay Raynor comments:

1

> Where are the right-wing voices who will take the establishment
> on? For decades, British theater has been dominated by
> playwrights sympathetic to a liberal consensus. The culture
> of the left has been represented by strident plays and angry
> playwrights, but where are the voices of the right, and why can't
> the stage accommodate both?[1]

Certainly, conservatism is not synonymous with plays that present a faith-based approach, but they are related in terms of themes offered up.

So, to solve the long-range problem, we need to train, prepare, mentor, and challenge more transformational artists to create within the purview of their worldview, and create works that will reflect the authenticity of their stance. This does not stand in opposition to good story, intricate structure, or complicated characterizations—for these are building blocks that all good story art is built on. Nor is it justified by creating stories that espouse only the virtues of right behavior inevitably leading toward happy endings.

As a practicing theater director and playwright in both the professional and academic arenas, I will articulate in this book some of the aesthetic and practical elements and thinking that have shaped my artistic expression. Thus, there are chapters that deal with the idea of the "beat" as the common denominator of expressive communication that the playwright uses as well as thoughts on the "creative mandate" and its ramifications. It is as much a memoir and a "How To" book as it is an exploration of elements and belief structures in the arts.

A primary purpose behind writing this book is to provide Christians with an approach for writing playscripts for the theater. I recognize that this might suggest niche writing, but in no instance, hopefully, does it compromise the presentation of the established writing techniques involved in the creation of character, plot, and structure developed by writers and portrayed on the stage over the centuries. And neither does it imply that the writer is only safe in producing biblically oriented drama or plays that are more concerned with soteriology, or the theology of salvation, than with good storytelling.

Part One of this book establishes some of the aesthetics of story and places the Christian writer within a more theoretical context. It begins in Chapter 1 with an overview on the nature and necessity of story in our lives and continues in Chapter 2 with just how theater as a genre exhibits its own storytelling attributes.

Chapter 3 addresses an observation that I have made in over forty years of teaching theater and film, and reflects on the question raised with sad regularity: "why do the preponderance of students I have taught over the years who classify themselves as Christians rarely try and integrate their faith experience and principles into their written creative work?" The challenges and stumbling blocks of developing a creative voice in terms of theatrical expression can be found in Chapter 4, "How Then Shall We Write," which puts forth some of the categories of faith and art that the writer can consider such as worldview, sin, image making, transcendence, change, destiny, and mystery, among others. Sources of the inspiration for the writer to consider will be presented ending in Chapter 5, Part One.

Part Two will feature the formalistic aspects of playwriting including character creation, premise, and structure, and ends with an overview of possible opportunities of writing for the market today. The Appendices will offer an array of essays that feature further discussion of aesthetics and script writing.

After each chapter there will also be discussion questions and exercises referencing the preceding material.

## Discussion Questions and Exercises

1. To what might you attribute the shortage of first-rate plays or movies presenting a faith-based context?

2. Provide examples in your opinion of both pro and con productions purporting to appeal to the Christian and church-affiliated audiences. What works for you and what does not?

# PART ONE

# Chapter 1

# Story

## *What It Is and How It Works*

THE ELEMENTS OF GOOD STORY have been well defined since the time of Aristotle, who wrote about tragedy as dramatic storytelling in his *Poetics* (c. 335 BCE). Since then, there has been no shortage of material on the subject. One can track through the ages the need for a good hook to help catch the attention of the audience or reader; the need for a variety of plot points which provide motivated changes for the protagonist; character arcs; progressive complications in the middle of the story; and a climax which provides "ah ha!" moments that were foreshadowed during the early parts of the story.

The protagonist should have a goal that is difficult to accomplish. She needs to contend with a personal flaw to accomplish the goal, and these challenges lead to enlightenment and potential change. Striving to reach the goal deals with testing positive and negative value systems, which is challenged by an antagonist who tries to prevent the above process from coming to fruition. Finally, then, theme is the result of this meaningful structured conflict. And if all these ingredients are working, a good story becomes a reality.

But the intricacies of plot point development are not the focus of this chapter. Rather, I will deal with the intrinsic value of story to us as artists and as individuals.

Anthropologists label us as *Homo sapiens,* meaning we stand erect with large brains and have developed language. Cultural theorist and historian Johan Huizinga has gone so far as to establish in his book *Homo Ludens* that we are distinguished from the species around us as being creatures of play.[1] Following Huizinga's example of categorizing our identity into more focused units, it may also be said that we are *homo fabulators,* or *homo historius,* or the tellers of significant events.

We learn early in Scripture (Gen. 1:27) that we are made in God's image. This makes us image makers ourselves. Our ability to communicate verbally and to write texts comes from this endowed gift. Through these mechanisms we can imagine and articulate, to a degree, the mysteries that surround us, including the reality of God himself through such linguistic devices as metaphor. What are the implications of being gifted with the title of metaphor-maker? Why is this so distinctive and necessary to the definition of who we are and what we can know?

First, it means that we are always seeking adjacent ways of explaining actions and environments. Why do we do this? Because we want to understand our existence: to feel it, to know it, and to personalize it. Why do we say a red, red rose is like . . . the universe? Because we want to recognize that we are not isolated in this creation, that we are organically connected, not only through cells and DNA and blood and air and water and earth, but also through meaning. Moreover, we recognize in the very connection itself that we are creating (or discovering) a deeper and more vivid description of what it means to exist. Metaphor-making is a way of cataloguing our experiences so they have personal meaning and go deeper than our understanding of physical principles. A theory explaining why waves occur and what they produce is fine, but why and how do we soar when we watch the waves on a stretch of deserted beach? A primary reason that we crave story is because it connects us emotionally and associatively with the world around us and allows us to imbue it with personal significance. American essayist and novelist Flannery O'Connor says:

> I have often asked myself what makes a story work, and what makes it hold up as a story, and I have decided that it is probably some action, some gesture of a character that is unlike any other in the story, one which indicates where the real heart of the story lies. This would have to be an action or a gesture which was both totally right and totally unexpected; it would have to be one that is both in character and beyond character; it would have to suggest both the world and eternity. The action or gesture I'm talking about would have to be on the anagogical level, that is, the level which has to do with the Divine life and our participation in it. It would be a gesture that transcended any neat allegory that might have been intended or any pat moral categories a reader could make. It would be a gesture which somehow makes contact with mystery.[2]

Aristotle notes that tragedy is an imitation of an action. But it is not just any action: it is an action that is pivotal, life changing, challenging, and loaded with potential meaning. These source moments are all around us. They can be found in a poet's description of a rose. Peter Shaffer reads a newspaper article about a boy who blinded some horses and creates the story of *Equus* (1967) in which a young man's personal angst results in a human cry for our need for mythic storytelling. Bertolt Brecht relates how a story happens. You see an accident. You are in shock. But it is only as you ruminate on the event that you begin to attribute motive and happenstance and irony and backstory and meaning to this chaotic happening so it can be passed on and made ultimate sense out of, both to you and those to whom you communicate.[3]

Jean Piaget, Nobel Prize winning child psychologist and author of the book *Play, Dreams, and Imitation in Childhood*, notes that one of the first impulses of the newborn baby is to mimic and to repeat actions in order that this may offer ways of accommodating ourselves to others and to our environment. We are constructed and defined in terms of what we want to emulate.[4] Storytelling does just that by offering narratives or paintings or dance or films that imitate, not exactly, but in ways that profoundly help us to understand who and why we feel the way we do and act. So this process of imitation is one which, when amplified through art, provides meaning and context that day-to-day life cannot. And, of course, this process of imitation stays with us throughout our lives. And for those who have embraced a faith in God's Son, we are on a constant journey of imitating Christ: "For you have been called for this purpose, since Christ also suffered for you, leaving you an example for you to follow in His steps" (1 Pet. 2:2, NASB).

In her seminal book *Feeling and Form: A Theory of Art*, Susanne Langer has commented that art is essentially giving form to feeling.[5] From the time that we are children, we are often victims of the chaotic bundle of feelings that seem to fill us to uncontrolled overflowing. As we get older, growing up, in large part, is learning how to redirect these feelings in a more acceptable way so they do not identify us or characterize us but instead communicate that we are in control when we are too often a mess inside. Art, by structuring emotion or feeling, provides a release. Aristotle calls this *catharsis*. By identifying with what the created character or moment is expressing emotionally, we find release from our own inner emotions.

Often as a director and writer I have stressed to my actors or young writers that an emotional moment must be earned and that it cannot be expressed without a careful cause-and-effect building of the moment. Otherwise, as an audience we are embarrassed, and we do not believe the moment as being truthful. We learn how to play against emotion because we know the power of its usage. It is something that is common to every culture. All people speak a similar language when it comes to emotion.

## Why We Need Story

Our need for story goes on. After watching the news, documentaries, and talk shows, I will turn to my wife and say, "I am ready for my fiction fix," or the need to cozy up with the right side of my brain, to lose myself in someone else's imagination. The big picture of our lives will fill a beginning-middle-end catalogue of experiences, but I am convinced that we need additional story input to experience this beginning-middle-end complex in more immediate terms. The continuum of our lives never quite gets to that dramatic end until it is literally almost all over. That is why we crave story, especially stories with definitive endings. How often have you judged a film or a novel by the way its narrative ends?

We hate stories that do not end. Our minds are constantly in a "what if" mode. We live inescapably in overlapping time warps—past, present, and future. The world for all of us is anchored with the "what if" questions as we see ourselves making different choices, exploring new ideas, or lamenting past mistakes. One of the exercises that I request of writing students is to take their character's present predicament and provide ten "what if" questions that explore new and more radical exigencies of behavior that could result in life changing events at any pivotal moment in the story.

I firmly believe that if the Genesis Fall had not happened, then our need for story would be greatly diminished. But it did. And it was when we were torn from our intimate relationship with our Creator and escorted from the garden that the existential questions of meaning and existence manifested themselves. These questions, at least structurally, can be addressed through story with its expression of endings. Every story has an eternal destiny. Each individual story cannot help but end the same way every time it is read or seen, and usually has a meaning as pieces get tied together and problems are resolved. We long for that same continuity of knowing who, where, and why that a good story provides, but which are missing to a degree as absolutes in our own lives.

*"Science, by its own definition, doesn't give us meaning. It just provides us with facts. Our lives gain meaning only when we tell our story."*[6]

—David Steindl-Rast

## Why Story Captivates

Stories highlight, explain, edify, and interpret aspects of our lives and our existence. What follows is a summary of why story captivates.

### Story Condenses Life and Gives It Meaning

The day-to-day wasting of time, energy, and thought is excluded from a good story—unless you venture into the existential. Currently, I am enjoying the television show *Bluebloods*. In the period of an hour, the show explores more actions and conflicts than I would probably experience in several decades of my life by featuring one main plot and at least three subplots interconnected and layered one top of the other.

### Story Provides Value Systems

Stories generally establish a moral or value-laden context, but through people and conflict and not through moral theorems or dictums. Thus, for the theme of "love your neighbor" (see Mark 12:30–31), Jesus chooses to explain this concept through the parable of the Good Samaritan. In other words, it appeals to us experientially through characters and actions that we can identify with and helps clarify the meaning of neighbor through actions, conflict, and choice.

### Story Provides a Meaningful Beginning, Middle, and End

Good stories take us on a ride like a roller coaster—slow builds, sudden descents, twists, turns, and thrills. Like the roller coaster there is a satisfying beginning and ending to each action. We know that it is going to end and that we will be safe. A good story often provides a structural answer to this psychological need. We long to be able to interpret our lives in terms of a good story, finding meaning and completeness throughout, ending with purpose and having fulfilled the assurance of "well done, good and faithful servant!" (Matt. 25:21, NIV). Too often we do not know why we are here, where we are going, and the purpose of our life escapes us. Scripture and its worldview provide a meaningful context to anchor this incompleteness, this longing for completion, which I think has been with us since the Fall. In John 8:14 (NKJV) Jesus says to the Pharisees, "Even if I bear witness of Myself, My witness is true, for I know where I came from and where I am going; but you do not know where I come from and where I am going." This implies that built into our life's venture is the ongoing search for our identity in the passage of time. Story reorders this loss by supplying the feeling of a surrogate's completion, at least for an aesthetic moment.

## Story Provides an Escape

Story vicariously offers a structured oasis in our often confused and complex lives by providing escape from boredom, from stress, and from worry. I think we crave the right brain experience whenever and wherever we can get it. Daydreaming is a practice we all indulge in that feeds this need. Three-minute web episodes based on a continuing romantic story offers the commuter audiences a brief break from the rituals of travel to and from work. Novels are getting shorter. The most successful television commercials oftentimes are mini-stories of characters finding happiness and connections in a 30-second narrative.

## Story Provides Affirmation of Tribal Traditions

Friedrich Nietzsche, in *The Birth of Tragedy* notes:

Every culture that has lost myth has lost, by the same token, its natural healthy creativity. Only a horizon ringed about with myths can unify a culture. The forces of imagination and the Apollonian dream are saved by myth from indiscriminate rambling. The images of myth must be the daemonic guardians, ubiquitous but unnoticed, presiding over the growth of the child's mind and interpreting to the mature man his life and struggles.[7]

Ongoing narratives often define community cohesiveness by codifying cultural identification. Note the great myths that evolve in almost all cultures, many of which have touchstones in historical happenings. Story is a way we know ourselves in the present by sharing a common heritage of stories from the past. These are the origin stories that help to define who we are or what we once were. These are the heroes that we have magnified and that provide the touchstones to our roots.

## Story Provides a Vehicle for Knowing Self and Others

Emotions in stories are the result of actions and impulses that we can identify with and say, "Yes, that's me." Or, "Yes, now I understand." It is the artistic impulse that gives ordered form to the expression of our emotional needs.

When we read a story or see a play, it is often the evolving life of the characters which enthrall us. How often have we gone to an action thriller—e.g., *Transformers* or a James Bond film—and come away exhilarated but still not quite full? We end up asking the question, "How did they do that?" rather than "Why did they do that?" We want to identify personally with the wants and needs of the characters. If elements of justification and motivation are missing in the character's arc, we feel that the story has been compromised.

When Robert McKee in his book *Story* emphasizes the need for progressive complication, he does not just mean the fabric of actions or plot which drive the character. Instead, he is referring to the ongoing sense of inner revelation that a good character depiction portrays, and which will ultimately lead to an Act Three climactic self-awareness.[8] Thus, when Hedda shoots herself at the end of Ibsen's classic masterpiece *Hedda Gabler* (1891), we believe it. We have the dawning revelation of how she has trapped herself through her own deception and ambition, and how she has no other choice but to end it all. We need communication with people to experience "otherness." We can do this through establishing relationships, but we can also bring this about vicariously by experiencing the creative mind of authors as well as the fictional characters they create. Jesus promised the coming of the Holy Spirit into our lives if we believe in and follow His way, and this represents a gifted expansion of the Old Testament way of communicating with God's otherness. We are accepting the invitation of God into our personal space through the Holy Spirit with the result, hopefully, being enhanced knowledge of Him and of ourselves and others. It is all relationally based.

Story is just one of the ways we can approach the attitudes and feelings of another person. How often have you felt personally violated through the depiction of a character in a story, or remain haunted by resultant imagery from a story viewed? The impulse for connection is always there. The resulting relationship can be compromised through the expression of perverse values that run counter to one's own. Some Christian denominations and families encourage a blanket rejection of stories created by the secular culture. It is perfectly understandable and even defensible for a Christian artist or audience member to refuse to watch or read certain questionable material. But to argue the aesthetic and value-oriented elements intelligently and meaningfully in these stories, you need to base your arguments and objections on the observation of the material in question. And this critical process will help establish, inform, and protect the viewer from swallowing secular worldviews unaware.

## The Connective Tissue of Story

While visiting an art exhibit at the Whitney Museum in New York City, I entered a large room that featured a huge canvas on one side that was all white and facing it on the opposite wall was an equal-sized canvas that was all black. I looked for different shadings, varied brush strokes, but could find no anomalies that would distinguish one painting from the other outside of the use of color. Interestingly, as I gazed at these uniform surfaces, I found myself manufacturing narratives that could possibly play themselves out against these backgrounds. I did the same a bit later with a painting by Jackson Pollack. I read into one of his turgid abstract expressionist works a story that would possibly have matched Pablo Picasso's "Guernica," with constructs that brought me back to my days as a soldier in Vietnam.

In the sixties I viewed Andy Warhol's film *Empire* (1964), which consists of a little over eight hours of continuous slow-motion footage of the Empire State Building in New York City. Audience members scoffed, yelled at the film, left in droves, mostly slept, but an interesting thing happened after about five hours of viewing this footage. On an upper floor of the building a light went on in one of the rooms. There was a stirring in the crowd. People speculated that someone was meeting for a late-night tryst; no, it was a janitor moving from room to room, and fledgling stories began to be birthed. We are so desperate for story that we will manufacture it from the most minimalist offerings to fill our daily quota of beginnings-middles-and-ends. While researching for a film I was writing about AIDS, my guide and friend Stephen Kuroswa—a Masai warrior and PhD student—introduced me to his brother, a chieftain of a small tribe outside of Longido,

Tanzania. But before this, he spent close to an hour reminiscing with his brother of their backgrounds together and bringing him up to date on his life as a student in the U.S. It was a non-stop monologue. And then his brother did the same thing back to him. The idea that they existed for each other through the continuity of word/memory/image, and that a quick "Hi, how are you" did not suffice, says something important about their community and its identity.

> *"Stories are at the very heart of being human;*
> *they talk about where we are from, where we are,*
> *and where we are going. They're like bread;*
> *you need to hear and tell them every day."*[9]
>
> —Bill Harley

In a play called *The Storyteller* (1998), a Fulani Hausa Prince—i.e., he has more than a dozen cows—becomes engaged to a White missionary woman in his native country of Nigeria. Though university educated, one of the roles he plays in his tribal unit is that of storyteller. The play begins as the engaged couple fly into Atlanta to have the wedding. It then shows how the Black and the White communities try to tear the pending marriage apart because the missionary woman comes from an old, White, and established southern family. What effect does a man who tells stories as his main contribution to society have on this divided culture? What can the power of story accomplish?

> *"An enemy is one whose story we have not heard."*[10]
>
> —Gene Knudsen Hoffman

As a Lieutenant in Vietnam in 1968–69, I began to realize that the war I was serving engaged two cultures that were essentially alien to each other. The U.S. military built huge complexes outside of Saigon which isolated large elements of the South Vietnamese and U.S. forces. The same thing happened in Cameron Bay, Danang, and Nah Trang. There was no attempt made to create any sort of symbiosis between the two cultures insofar as language, history, social structure, or art were concerned.

The U.S. essentially joined the war to ameliorate the domino effect of having all of Asia going communist if the civil war in the country was not won by the South Vietnamese. The "story" of the conflict between North and South Vietnam goes back thousands of years. Peter Weiss, German author and creator of *Marat/Sade* (1963) wrote a play titled *Discourse on the Progress of the Prolonged War of Liberation in Vietnam and the Events Leading Up to It as Illustration of the Necessity for armed Resistance Against Oppression and on the Attempts of the United States of America to Destroy the Foundations of Revolution* (1968). Perhaps if the powers that be could have read and understood what Weiss relates about the relationship of the two social and tribal substrata in this small Asian country, then the American catastrophe of Vietnam may have been avoided. The U.S. had no idea of what the story had been, was, or was going to be. Is story, then, the panacea that will ultimately bring about world peace? Probably not. But understanding the differences as well as the similarities between cultures honestly portrayed through story could certainly help the process of "loving one's neighbor" (see Mark 12:30–31).

## Story and the Cultural Context

If one looks at the rise and fall of civilizations based on their artistic output, there are some interesting distinctions to note. In comparing the artistic output of Athens and Sparta during the fifth century, one can see the difference between a democracy and a militaristic state. Sparta is known today for the Battle of Thermopylae, Marathon, and a host of others. But where is their contribution to humanistic thought? It is almost nonexistent. Athens is known today for its contribution to epic poetry, architecture, and serving as the crucible where western drama (tragedy and comedy) were birthed. Roman civilization is noted for its absorption of art from the countries that it conquered and much of its academic and artistic output was absorbed from Greek culture. The flowering of Renaissance art in Italy, France, and especially England became the expression of societies that were essentially adventurous, and which established enlightened statehoods that sponsored and supported artistic effort. There is a history of state support of the arts which resulted in remarkable flowering of unique and individualized expression. Am I implying that state funding of the arts is a positive phenomenon?

Government support of the arts is by no means a contemporary phenomenon. The great poetry and dramatic contests of ancient Greece, which gave birth to the plays of Aeschylus, Sophocles, and Euripides, were state funded. So were the productions of Plautus and Terrance in Rome.

The marvelous medieval pageants that depicted God's Creation through the Second Coming of Jesus Christ shared expenses between the municipal governments and the working guilds. Renaissance drama companies were supported by top government officials, and the extravagant masques of Elizabeth's and James I's reigns were state funded. Louis IV was known as supporting sumptuous architectural constructs as well as musical composers. In Taiwan, the great tradition of the Peking Opera is supported with three separate companies under the control of the Air Force, the Army, and the Navy. In England, since the 1950s the great resurgence of new dramatists and musicals on the London stage and the regions happened simultaneously with the creation of the Arts Council. This organization, which is administered primarily by professional artists, aids across the whole spectrum of the arts, from underwriting losses to developing artist-in-residence programs.

In the U.S. during the Depression, the Works Progress Administration supported and encouraged the work of poets, dramatists, and musicians. Jackson Pollack and Saul Bellow (to name just two) received federal support during these years, as did Arthur Miller, Tennessee Williams, and Orson Welles from the Federal Theater Project. Where would the state of the arts in the U.S. be had the original impetus and phenomenal grass roots productivity of this period not been continued by the federal government? The present Endowment programs for the Humanities and the Arts were started under the Johnson administration and grew to full flower under the Nixon presidency.

Where totalitarian and repressive regimes exist, too often the expression of the arts is used as a tool of the state, and individual expression is seriously compromised unless individuals submit to the state's propaganda dictums. The Nazis sought an external form that posited a racial ideal. Thus, they looked toward Roman and Greek perfect forms as representing an art form that was uncontaminated by the Jewish culture. Erwin Piscator, Bertolt Brecht, and many other artists fled for their lives from Nazi repression. Russian socialist realism provided a thin covering of masking propaganda as art. I love the Chinese Opera form with its masks, costumes, and acrobatics, but when Mrs. Mao labeled it as decadent and had the artists performing in peasant garb and military grays, it lost its soul, just like the people. One can often gauge a country's state of repression by using a cultural barometer as to what is allowed and what is banned in the artistic arena. In Eastern Europe before the Berlin wall was destroyed, productions of *Measure for Measure* (c. 1604) by William Shakespeare were in vogue because of its implied statement of what happens to a government when its citizens lose their personal freedoms.

## Art and the Corruption of the Imagination

Up to this point, the use of story has been proposed as a positive cultural phenomenon. But as Genesis 6:5 (NIV) notes: "Yahweh saw that the wickedness of man was great in the earth, and that every imagination of the thoughts of man's heart was continually only evil."

The idea or concept of an "evil" or "sick" imagination is with us today in the plethora of morally corrupt (by biblical standards) film and narrative literature. Addiction to pornography is more rampant than alcoholism. It cripples healthy sexual relationships between men and women and promotes degradation and objectification—to say nothing of its perverse abuse of children in the presentation of sexual license.

In Noah's day, the culture most likely indulged their imaginations without restriction. In a culture that has no "God resonance," this means that every possible immoral extension or use of imagery and our bodies is capitalized on. When left to itself, imagination becomes the plaything of the forces of darkness. Look at our current technological revolution: private movies on demand; buds in our ears that tune everything else out and let anything in; social media projections of personal sexuality; sexual robots that cater to every want and desire; and unwholesome films and television series that praise and contribute to the onslaught of sexual mores and imagery. Computer games encourage and cultivate fields of killing and acquisition of fighting weapons as a primary goal. My fourteen-year-old grandchild is projected onto an island with a hundred other virtual players, and they battle it out until there is a handful left standing at the end of the killing.

We have created a highly entertaining, completely immersive world of constantly shifting images, many of which draw their inspiration from the occult, or various violent scenarios. We can kill at will and pay no price. We can indulge in sexual fantasies and feel no shame and especially avoid all responsibility. I believe we are in a period of mass hardening of the heart in which we accept and normalize the most violent and morally degraded behavior at the cost of our personal sensitivity and soulfulness, and which is canonized by state and local governments as permissible. But who is writing a fictional and morally negative response to such phenomena?

As Christians we represent a minority, a counter-cultural phenomenon that is labeled as politically incorrect; as hate "speech"; as racist; as discriminatory; as judgmental; as retro-everything; and ultimately as fascist. What can we do to counter this pervasive onslaught of condemnation and ultimate rejection? (The suggested answers to this question below supplement the various ideas and concepts put forth in Chapter 4: "How Then Shall We Write?")

To begin, since we as Christians know a spiritual reality, we need to reveal and substantiate this reality by creating works that expand beyond *literalism* or *realism*—the latter being defined as depicting the here and now in essentially linear terms. If we pursue the metaphysical implications of living in multiple realities—just as we sit in a physical location to write while our mind grapples with past imagery, with fantasy, with altering reality, and with future projections—perhaps we can produce works that will challenge our audiences, that will be unique, and that will capture the mystery of the epic saga which begins with Creation and continues through to the coming of the Kingdom.

I think that bringing our spiritual sensibilities in imaginative ways to the various genres of storytelling is a way to enhance our offerings to the dominant culture. Science fiction, fantasy, and horror genre films flirt with our innate responsiveness to the "otherness" of our present existence. Exploring this subject matter in terms of a "God awareness" would offer questions and even solutions to humankind's query, "Is this it, or is there something more?" If demons can possess human beings, then where are the angels that defend us? Could a search for the Ark of the Covenant result in something more than a *Raiders of the Lost Ark* (1981) finale of God being packed away in a crate in a government warehouse? C. S. Lewis provides a taste of what can be done in fantasy through his Narnia books. He provides a trip to heaven and hell in *The Great Divorce* (1945) and introduces us to devilish plotting in *The Screwtape Letters* (1942). Other notable contributions are *The Lord of the Rings* (1955) by J. R. R. Tolkien; *The Book of the Dun Cow* (1978) by W. Wangerin Jr.; *Dragon King Trilogy* (1982–1984) by Steve Lawhead; *The Golden Key* (1867) by George Macdonald; *This Present Darkness* (1986) by Frank Peretti; and *The Circle Series* (2004–2009) by Ted Dekker. But the novel form seems to be far ahead of the stage or media in scope, richness, and quality of its offerings. Significant and challenging works dealing with spiritual issues based on a biblical context are needed in the dramatic arts.

I think that the church has reneged on its responsibilities to nurture and promote creative talent in the faith-based arena. Scholarships are given to ministry and mission students, but where is the church that is sponsoring artists-in-residence, and then performing their works? Willow Creek Church outside of Chicago had drama and music offerings that spearheaded the use and publication of the dramatic sketch, monologue, and full-blown musicals for years. I assisted in the writing of a feature length original musical titled *Jairus* that sold 40,000 tickets before the opening night's performance in 2000. Unfortunately, their impetus in this area has diminished.

In addition to the church, the vast array of private Christian colleges and universities often consider theater training, including play and film script writing, to be peripheral and luxury items in their curriculum. Facilities are often substandard, programs staffed with adjuncts, and even then, vastly understaffed. Funding is minimal, and the schools rarely take the risk of producing new work by emerging artists.

A paradigm that would enhance the creation of new works would look something like this: a private Christian university hosts a national playwriting contest; the winner's script is produced in the subsequent season by the institution. The writer is brought in for a pre-production development stage as an artist-in-residence during the preparation of the play and its production. This writer could contribute by teaching workshops or shortened courses while in residence. The play is staged, and professional theater directors are flown in to evaluate the play as part of the process of considering it for production. The play is picked up and given a professional production at a regional theater. Both the school and the playwright have benefited and contributed to the growth of artists and artistic material in the culture. Regent University's Theater program invited a Canadian playwright, Dennis Hassell, to workshop and produce as part of the regular season his new play *Glory Man* (2009), which is the story of Clarence Jordon (who wrote *Cotton Patch Gospel*, 1981) and his efforts in the 1950s to start a racially mixed commune in the deep south. Directors were flown in from around the country and the play was later produced by The Lamb's Players in San Diego. It is presently being considered for a film rendition. From writer to small college, to professional theater, to possible filmic rendering: a model to be emulated.

I personally believe that we are in, or approaching, the end times, considering its depiction in Scripture, cf. Daniel, Ezekiel, Revelation, and the Gospels. If this is true, an informed and even urgent response should be a much-needed subject for faith-based writers. The film version of *Left Behind* (2000) offered a mediocre product. The media are inundated at this time with films and novels that depict a catastrophic dystopian view of the end times as we can imagine it. But the Christian corollaries to this are too often sadly neglected.

So, too, with the vampire craze: our archetypal longing for immortality or living forever is featured in television series and films and novels. The true answer and response to this longing that can be found in the redemptive work of Jesus Christ is rarely featured. Why? Partly because it has become cheapened and ridiculed by a world that has little response to the urgency of an end times' call or concept of salvation. Climate change is a secular parallel. On March 9, 2019, the House of Representatives passed a non-binding resolution condemning all hate speech used against a slew of Eastern religions, including Judaism, but neglected to include Christianity, which is regularly lambasted on late night talk shows and even by U.S. Senators. Christianity is no longer revered, or its theology appreciated as it proclaims the one and only path to the Father in Heaven. Rather, it has become an embarrassment and a politically incorrect cultural anomaly. Redemptive art that resonates can help to address and change this sad situation.

Our need for story then is the need to return to the child-like (not childish) heroic adventure to save one in peril, in danger of pain, suffering, loss, and ultimately eternal death. And to experience, to some degree, an indescribable sense of His presence, His joy, and love.

Story, thus, is the ultimate means not by which we escape from reality, but by which we make sense of reality so that we can cope with the natural tendencies of this universe, this existence, whose forces conspire to render our plight hopeless and thus meaningless. Story, at its highest is the relative experience of Christ "who for the joy set before Him endured the cross, despising the shame, and has sat down at the right hand of the throne of God" (Heb. 12:2, NASB). And for us human beings it extends beyond coping, no, not only extends but delves as if in a desperate search for breath in a vacuum. Michael Torres notes in *God's Story Structure*: "And this is even more greatly pronounced as a struggle, literally, between life and death, between the forces of light and darkness, our nature as made in the image of God and made of dust."[11]

## Discussion Questions and Exercises

1. Take any three Aesop's Fables. These are some of the earliest stories passed down over the centuries. What do you see in them that causes them to work as effective stories?

2. When you were a child, hopefully your parents read to you from the array of children's literature. What stories do you remember wanting to hear repeatedly? As story, what would you say makes these so appealing? You can respond to this personally as well as commenting on the story elements that you feel attributed to the success of you as a responder.

3. Your favorite story genre might be fantasy, or detective thrillers, or horror. What is it about your favorite story genre that appeals to you? How do you feel it accomplishes this? Provide a list of story elements that you feel make this genre work for you.

4. As a Christian, do you feel called to write stories that reflect your personal religious ethos? If so, what do you want to avoid in terms of articulating possible faith elements? If not, why not?

5. Describe a moment in your life history that dramatically changed you. Include specific descriptions of actions, dialogue, imagery, and environment. Do you sense in this a possible story origin? What would you do to make it universally empathetic to a much larger audience?

# Chapter 2

# What Is Theater?

THORNTON WILDER, AMERICAN DRAMATIST, REMARKS:

> I regard the theater as the greatest of all art forms, the most immediate way in which a human being can share with another the sense of what it is to be a human being. This supremacy of the theater derives from the fact that it is always "now" on the stage.[1]

The composer needs to be aware of a wide range of musical notes and chord applications as well as instrumental possibilities before she can write music. The poet must be familiar with rhythmic line and verse usages that create intense imagery and how these elements are different from the narrative or media expression of language. The dancer records and passes on dance sheets which have captured much of the intricacy of step progression. My father was a professional artist and he spent extensive training in studying anatomy and the drawing of hands, feet, and skin tones, all necessary foundational techniques to master before he launched into his oil painting career.

And so it is with the theater. Some of the artistic elements the playwright must master are imagining a story that evolves in a three-dimensional environment; mastering emotional builds and story progression; being a student of suspense; learning the economy of writing for an already created space; being aware of prop usages; and understanding the intricacies of dialogue as it relates to character.

*Theater* is a live performance executed by people for people that presents a series of meaningful dramatic or conflictual events presented in an illusory manner. *Drama* is the story or script to be enacted. Theater is thus the performance of that drama or play.

Do you need a script to have a theater performance? No. Theater can be totally nonverbal. It can also be 100% improvisational.

Do you need a stage to have a theater performance? No. In the National Theater's production of the *Medieval Mystery Plays* (1999), the space used was an empty warehouse, with the audience moving between dramatic elements, while the actors created vignettes in different areas. The audience was "in the round" and mobile. Street Theater is done in the street. Nightclubs, church basements, gymnasiums, classrooms, graveyards, and cathedrals all have served as theater spaces for different productions I have attended.

The type of play, the nature of audience interaction, the size of the company, the financial considerations, and much more contribute to the choice of space/audience relationships. What is the effect on the writer? William Shakespeare wrote for the Globe Theater, among others, and the thrust stage arrangement meant that he had to write exit and entrance lines of a certain length to help get the actors on and off stage. A small company in Austin, Texas, the Third Course Theater under the direction of Lisa Neely, takes their performances into living rooms with an audience that is merely a handful. The nature of this drama is going to be intimate, even confessional. I wrote part of my doctoral dissertation on the effect that writing for theater-in-the-round had on a group of English playwrights who came to work at the Victoria Theater in Stoke on Trent, a professional arena stage company. I was interested to discover how the introduction of a new spatial form began to affect what they could write and where they could go in terms of aesthetic choices when compared with the proscenium stages that they were accustomed to. I found their work became more scenically fluid, with far more exploration of locations and an expanded mindset that was open to theatrical possibilities.

## Live Theater: What Is the Appeal?

Watching live actors on stage, we realize that they are presenting themselves with no buffers to protect themselves: they could drop a line, the lights could go out, or the audience might not laugh when they are supposed to. In other words, it is a situation fraught with a sense of risk: in fact, the stress factor on an actor on opening night exceeds that of a test jet pilot on an initial test flight. This contributes to a sense of community as the audience finds joy and comfort in the fact that they cannot only see and experience the live presence of an actor who is risking all for them, but also that the actor is responding to them. Film has no equivalent to Shakespeare's soliloquies, one-person shows, or musical comedy singing numbers where direct eye contact is a reciprocal process with the audience.

It should be noted that live theater is always happening in the present and no two performances are ever quite the same. In their production of *The Fight for Shelton Bar* (1974), a musical docu-drama which depicts the history and productivity of the steel mills in the Midlands, the Victoria

Theater was trying to save the mill from Prime Minister Thatcher's policy of closing all inland steel companies in England. Each night they updated the show with actors presenting snippets of news articles and interviews that would impact the outcome. In the musical *The Mystery of Edwin Drood* (1985), the audience is canvassed and decides who is guilty of the murder as part of the Act Three climax. Performance theater, or experimental theater, is usually defined in terms of variant audience-performer relationships during the production. I have also authored several children's theater plays that are participatory, that is, they invite the audience to get out of their seats and to make a difference in the action by going on stage.

While in a graduate seminar on Play, Ritual, Sports, and Theater Dynamics taught by Richard Schechner, the corollaries between these performance entities were analyzed, and one of the more interesting comparisons was with ritual. If one looks at the attributes of ritual and theater, then a means of defining what theater is becomes more identifiable. Both ritual and theater have communication as their legacy: ritual vertically toward God, and theater horizontally toward the community of humankind. Both are designed in some fashion to try and change or influence their audiences with a message. Theater and ritual are both performed in a special arena of presentation; both ascribe a special significance to the symbolic use of objects or props; both usually require special costuming; both use repetition, saying and doing the same thing repeatedly; and both use highly select and energized language. Both are theatrical in that they use established conventions that are stylized statements about reality. (The idea of what theatrical means and how it works will be discussed later in this chapter.)

Theater is supposed to create an illusion and uses fabricated story to try and communicate some sort of truth. Ritual would deny this fabricated story nature in its truth-seeking purpose. Ritual might describe its practice, communion, for example, to be based on prior history and have story elements but would deny being involved in the manufacture of fictive illustrations. An attempt of bringing the two worlds together was evident in the Living Theater's production of *Frankenstein*, which was performed in Cincinnati's Playhouse in the Park, in the late 1960s. As the audience assembled, the Company of actors were sitting on the stage, chanting, burning incense, and performing what looked like a ritual enactment as they attempted to make the actor in their midst levitate. The audience sat there, waiting, for half an hour or so both before and after the curtain went up. Then the drama began because the ensemble was unable to get the actor to levitate, with said actor becoming the character of Frankenstein as a kind of punishment, and the show proceeded. What would have happened if the actor had levitated? The show would have ended. Reality, even though a miracle, brings fantasy to a halt.

In a production I directed of *Hamlet* (c. 1600) at the Three Rivers Shakespeare Festival in 1988, in the final duel between Hamlet and Laertes, Hamlet's poniard went flying into the audience and hit some elderly lady in the head. The actor playing Hamlet, Rick McMillan, leapt into the audience to see how she was, obviously breaking the illusory nature of the show. Apologies were made and the show resumed after the accident was addressed.

Theater is a live performance prescribed within certain time limits that translates out of this time. In other words, it has a beginning-middle-and-end, like a football game, and could cover twenty years, but take just two hours to perform. It is not life. And unlike a football game one is not likely to be injured. What about reality television shows such as *Survivor*? If you look at it and others like it closely, you can see, through editing, the emergence of a rough three-act structure. It purports to be like real life but features an island as a performance space, a series of athletic competitions, ongoing conflict between performers and teams, and ritualistic devices that offer survival rewards.

## Theater is Composed of Conflictual Events

You may be familiar with the truisms of what makes up conflict in literary works: conflict within people; conflict between people; conflict between man and nature or his environment; and conflict between humans and God. Tension, stress, suspense, progressive conflicts, and antagonists all provide the obstacles for the goals that every protagonist must endure and hopefully conquer. Conflict is the major ingredient in launching your central character on her goal-oriented journey, in creating believable exposition scenes, and in sustaining suspense. Without these conflictual elements, you might have a commentary or a real-life depiction, but you will probably not hold an audience.

Through events the conflict is shaped in a dramatic manner with certain plot points that drive forward the story, or the wants and needs of the characters. Examples of meaningful events in drama are Hamlet meeting the ghost in *Hamlet*; King Lear banishing Cordelia in *King Lear* (c. 1606); and Willy Loman committing suicide in *Death of a Salesman* (1949). These events are related through cause and effect and reflect on the nature of who we are as people and address the questions of how we should live or die.

## Theater is Performed in an Illusory Manner

By *illusory* I mean that the reality of time, space, character, and action is fictionalized. We pretend that we are in another time. We try and make 1904 happen on stage in Anton Chekhov's *The Cherry Orchard* (1904). But as theater approaches existential themes, the sense of time is even more violated. In *Waiting for Godot* (1952), Gogo and Didi are in a timeless state. Rhythms are substituted for career sequencing, implying that emotional and physical moments can happen arbitrarily outside of the cause-and-effect nature of related happenings. Characters have no identifiable back-story. They have no history to relate to and no jobs to define them. Not even the release of dying is a factor. They exist in an undefinable wasteland of in-betweenness. Perhaps Samuel Beckett has hit upon a way to express the existential angst of contemporary human beings filling up time that has lost its meaning and hope, creating these two unforgettable characters who are waiting, and waiting some more, but for what? For God, perhaps?

### The Illusory Nature of Time

The time that the play takes is illusory time—except in such works as *A Long Day's Journey into Night* (1939) by Eugene O'Neill or to a degree, Edward Albee's *Who's Afraid of Virginia Woolf* (1966)—but only if you take away the intermissions. So in Shakespeare's *A Midsummer Night's Dream* (c. 1596), in two hours we experience four lovers' night long venture in the woods. Or in Bertolt Brecht's *Mother Courage and Her Children* (1946), we journey with Mother Courage through episodic moments of the Hundred Years War. We have flashbacks, in Tennessee Williams's telling of *The Glass Menagerie* (1944), through Tom Winfield's recollections; and in Harold Pinter's *Betrayal* (1978), the entire play is run backwards so that the last scene of the play is presented first and then proceeds back in time in successive scenes to the first scene of the play. A terrible irony results. On stage we are always in another time, a made-up time, a time that is either in the past or the future; also, a time that is highly selective in that we watch just the actions which will best portray the conflict and growing tension of the evolving story line.

## The Illusory Nature of Space

If you took a window washer and you put him on a stage with his equipment and set up a dirty window, as real as he might perform his cleaning duties, he would not be fifty feet in the air. He would not be outside, and he would be conscious of an audience watching his every move. By taking the activity of washing a window out of its spatial matrix, you are creating the illusion of another space. This space can be made expressionistic with lights and projections, but we are always reminded that the workman is "playing" at washing windows. He will not drop fifty feet if he falls unless it is mimed in some stylized capacity. David Belasco's realistic theatrical environments in *The Governor's Lady* (1912) featured a working duplication of Julia Child's restaurant complete with gas and running water. But still, this naturalism does not allow for a culinary experience or a crowded restaurant outside the stage kitchen doors. Theater space can be organic, evolving, or even mimed. The mime artist lifts his hands and hunches down as he feels rain. We are encouraged to imagine real rain.

So we create the illusion of a space, a space appropriate to best tell the story. It can be symbolic. The set for *Good* (1982) by C. P. Taylor used the shape of the star of David in the floor construction. In a production by the Ibsen Foundation in Pittsburgh of *The Doll's House* (1985), as Nora disassociates herself from her domestic bungalow, the realistic set is stripped of furniture. It can also be metaphorical in the way the Kit Kat Club in *Cabaret* (1966) stands for the 1930s Berlin pre-WW2 decadence.

## The Illusory Nature of Character

The actor in a theater production is playing as truthfully as possible another person/character existing in another time and place. The actor must be "in the moment" and must identify with his character to understand the character's objectives, goals, and needs. He must be skilled enough in the presentation that a live audience will believe in him and the story.

## The Illusory Nature of Action

Aristotle in his *Poetics* notes that tragedy is an imitation of an action. By action he is implying more than just imitating some housewife doing the dishes at night or someone pushing a stroller through the park. These imitated actions must be highly selective and denotative. They have to be the best action for the moment, the actions that will reveal what the characters are made of, what the characters want, and how the characters go after getting it. This action is tied to the dramatic structure, an evolving plan of progressive complications that make life for our protagonist more difficult and challenging. There must also be a truthful representation of the theme, the character, and the action.

In *Oedipus Rex* (429 BC), Oedipus sets off to heal the city of Thebes from the curse of the plague. He is not a chimney sweep; he has been made King. He must contend with high officials, with prophets, and with striking political, family, and prophetic events that culminate in his self-immolation. We do not expect such actions from Gus in *The Dumbwaiter* (1957) or from Felix in Neil Simon's *The Odd Couple* (1965). The actions must be earned. Medea's lament and fury at the end is caused by rejection after rejection that has led her to kill her own children. An action that is earned is an action that derives from the truthful relationship of form or structure to content or idea. Aristotle was dealing primarily with the idea of tragedy, where the outcome is the result of what happens when personal pride bumps up against God's requisites. How, when, where, and why Oedipus brings about his own destruction provide the measuring sticks for the nature of the action in terms of tragedy. *Death of a Salesman* is a tragedy because Willy Loman's life is symbolic of a vast repository of lost souls in contemporary American life who have no direction, no moral foundation, and little family relevance. As Willie's wife notes after his suicide, "attention must be paid." I question whether the actions of this play or the nature of the characters merits the label of tragedy. It is pathetic and moving but falls short of the tragic actions played out in *Oedipus Rex*. Oedipus is a King who is torn from his throne and whose self-banishment becomes necessary for saving the Kingdom from the plague. Willy's death is secreted away in a basement as he sucks gas, a life wasted. It is a life compromised by small-time ambitions that were never realized because of Willy's adultery with prostitutes and his irrational mental state.

So returning to the initial question posed in this chapter: is opera theater? Yes, it has all the elements previously outlined. What about a football game? What about a rock concert? What about a courtroom trial? In the circus, the animal trainer might be wearing a special costume, he might have props such as a whip and chair, but what he is doing is real. The lion could eat him; the elephant could trample him. He is a trainer both on stage and off.

## Matrix and Non-Matrixed Categorization

A matrixed story construction adheres to the illusory elements involved in dramatic construction and realization. In neo-classic terms this would be labeled as adhering to the unities of time, place, and action. When these aspects of the illusory or conflictual nature of theater are broken or absent, the play moves from being a matrixed to a non-matrixed performance. Examples can be found in such quasi-theatrical experiences as happenings, street theater, and other improvisational constructs. *Happenings* purposefully violate the essential logic of a cause-and-effect progression of a story. An example would be where one shows up at an exhibition hall in which attendees walk on various canvas circular pieces. Depending on what color they are on determines what musical instrument they will try and play. The result could be a nostalgic, moving chord or complete musical chaos. *Street theater* can feature costumes, characterization, and isolated bits of programmed action designed to excite reactions from the audience. But aesthetic coherence is often dependent upon chance environmental constraints and audience interaction.[2]

In more structured dramatic experiences such as *Waiting for Godot*, the story is constructed around waiting and instead of a progressively building plot line that moves a story forward, ritual repetitive actions are enacted to fill up time. The audience is exposed to the experience of existential despair through personal boredom in having to endure a theatrical event that denies developed story viability.

## Theatrical Conventions

If the writer can grasp the concept of theatrical conventions, he is well on his way to mastering the particular and unique aspects that define the genre of drama. The following looks at how to stage the idea of transcendence through an examination of the use of theater conventions.

The final page of Lucia Frangione's playscript *Espresso* (2004) reads as follows:

> ROSA: Where is Dad now? Tony? Perhaps the next life will be a
> better life and that is something still to hope for. It's all we're going to
> get. It is such an immense mystery. How can I believe that my spirit
> and all my good might separate from my bad when my body dies,
> like oil separates from water and rises into eternity?

AMANTE: The winter is past; the rains are over and gone; the season of singing has come.

ROSA: Nonna and I go to Israel in the spring, the last spring we have together before she dies. We see Bethlehem. We walk the road of Golgotha. And we float in the dead sea.

> (*AMANTE buoys her up and lifts her, she gasps with the rush of it and outstretches her arms as eagles are heard above.*)[3]

The above represents what I would define as a transcendent moment which is communicated through lyrical language, a nonrealistic physical epiphany, and accompanying sound that suggests that stirring passage from Isaiah: "they shall mount up with wings like eagles" (Is. 40:31, NRSV). It is a theatrical moment conveyed using theatrical conventions. By conventions I mean the rules established by the playwright introduced early in the drama. In *Espresso*, for example, the use of two actors who play a multiplicity of characters, including spiritual or angelic representations, is established from the play's onset. I contend that the creative choices which characterize this final scene from *Espresso*, the realization of a transcendent moment using theatrical conventions, is an aspect of playmaking that is neglected as part of the creative vocabulary of many contemporary Christian dramatists.

The *theatrical convention* is the way in which time and space is manipulated on the stage. Pseudolus sings to and addresses his audience in *A Funny Thing Happened on the Way to the Forum* (1962). He has broken the illusion of a separate time and space between audience and play. He is talking to us. But this comic intimacy is lost when Zero Mostel in the film version talks to the camera.

These conventions are more than just tools to transform space and time. Because they are representative of a greater reality, they oftentimes become symbolic of a character's state of mind. I return to Frangione's *Espresso* in which the actress playing Rosa takes on the roles of several of Rosa's female relatives. This is more than just a display of theatrical virtuosity. The character of Rosa is haunted by these other characters, at times obsessed with them; they are a part of her, so the convention of being transformed into multiple characters becomes a psychologically meaningful ploy.

Most sketches performed in churches, at retreats, and in schools lack the use of meaningful theatrical conventions. Incorporating them could move these mini dramas beyond the realm of domestic soap operas to contend with themes and images and faith questions of a far broader range, as well as provoking and challenging audiences with conventions that cause them to expand their imaginations. This is not to say that well-performed realistic drama cannot be effective—it can. But as spiritual beings and as artists we are cognizant that we live in two worlds simultaneously—the unseen and the seen. How to express this dual reality becomes the challenge: maintaining the lyrical mystery of our existence without trivializing it.

For the theater to flourish, I believe that the reawakened imagination of the playwright must create dramas that engage the contemporary angst of our culture in a manner that is exclusive to the theater. I am talking here of dramas that embrace the potent reality that we live in a moral universe, that we are capable of transcendence, and that we are not bound by material reality (which is the purview of film). To better understand how this can be accomplished, it is first necessary to understand the basic nature of the theatrical in theater.

Theater is artifice and it should not pretend to be something that it is not. It should not try to convince us that we are being transported into a realistic world that mirrors what we see around us. It is artificial. What we see around us is not the sum of who we are as human beings in this universe. But this is nothing new. The Greeks, Shakespeare, and later the symbolists and expressionists at the turn of the last century were adherents of this viewpoint.

To the degree that theater becomes true metaphysical play in creating moments and worlds that go beyond the material depiction of reality, I find it most fascinating. We expand our existential boundaries because we are asking the audience to expand theirs by stretching the limits of their imaginations. More, rather than less, becomes possible using challenging theatrical conventions, and what is so important is that we are creating stories in such a way that they defy the depictions of reality so prevalent in film. We cannot compete with the image-making process of a film. But when two actors walk out on a bare stage, one Cain and the other Abel, and we watch as one symbolically breaks the back of his brother over his knee, the idea of the introduction of death into our history becomes more archetypal. It becomes more elemental than showing a filmed version of Cain and Abel surrounded by a jungle environment with all the realistic background accessories that come with it.

The belief we live in a universe sustained by an all-knowing, all-loving God is the starting point for denying an exclusively materialistic outlook on life. The theater I am prescribing is one that posits the possibility of multi-levels of reality. In realistic theater we can talk about ourselves as spiritual beings. In the theater of artifice and radical conventions we can express our story physically through movement, sound, and abstraction in a likeness to the otherness of the spiritual world that surrounds us.

God made us metaphor-makers because he wants to provide us with a means to approach the mystery of his Being. It is a part of the "creative mandate." The more realistic or static our artwork, the more our image making is dulled or reduced, and the less our imaginations are challenged. We should not attempt to hide the rules of our pretend game but should instead celebrate that the source of our reality is the physical, live presence of the actor, the presence of the audience and the assurance that truth can be contained in artifice. In other words, at the same time we know the actor in his fictive role is a liar, we simultaneously acknowledge that he speaks and acts great truth. Theater can only thrive if these elements of artifice are praised, not looked upon as shortcomings. In this way we can hope to deal with making an image of the transcendent a palpable artistic reality on the stage without losing its mysterious qualities through literalism or cheap special effects.

A professional writer recently described her work as Christian in that it had a redemptive ending, touting a meaningful moment of forgiveness as justification for the work and for her understanding of how to articulate her faith on the stage. There is nothing wrong with this but plays by Christian writers have no monopoly on redemptive themes. The world regularly produces works that are morally redemptive, full of forgiveness, healing, second chances, and love. What is more challenging from an aesthetic standpoint are the attempts by creative artists to depict aspects of spiritual reality on the stage. The presence of the ineffable and how it is communicated usually involves the use of concrete theatrical conventions. The danger is this can be sentimental, condescending, and predictable. Or on the other hand it can be provocative, challenging, and mysterious.

Flannery O'Connor suggests that to make the supernatural real we must first make the natural world supercharged with significant reality. She discusses finding the "moment of grace" which is often expressed in a gesture that is completely within character, but beyond character, organic to the moment and yet wholly unexpected, and so creating a moment that touches mystery. O'Connor borrows from theology the idea of an image that speaks on multiple levels, and she is particularly interested in attempting to express what she terms the "anagogical level"—or that which expresses the Divine life and our participation in it in a way that is expressed through the numinous rather than the phenomenal.[4]

To realize this last form of transcendence will require an intimate knowledge of human character and how the human reaches for the ineffable. It will need conventions that abstract human thought and action without losing its wellspring in the immediately physical.

So we return to the final image with which we began this discussion, from the play *Espresso*. Rosa is lifted by an angel or Christ figure. But the angel is an actor. And the angel/actor sweats. And the angel/actor is not wearing wings or carrying a harp. She circles the stage on his back, she does not fly off, but she is transported. And so are we.

## Why Do I Love the Theater?

I love the theater because it is my way of tinkering with the mystery that we are all living in, whether we want to admit it or not. In theater we create meaning out of transition and gestural moments; we work with artifice that suggests there is always more; we communicate truths horizontally to the audience which bridge the gap vertically with the intimate Other. I am fascinated with theoretical aspects of quantum physics which strive to define a new cosmological relationship between energy, matter, and motion mysteriously revealed in the universe. It is postulated that the same electron can be in two different places at the same time. Mind blowing. But how much like that is our existence as believers in an infinite God? We exist in this material world while at the same time are in-dwelt with the Spirit and seated in heavenly places (Eph. 2: 4-7). In other words, like an electron, we can exist in two different worlds simultaneously. Our challenge as playwrights is finding how to encapsulate in a story the structural and thematic anomalies of this space/time mystery.

## Discussion Questions and Exercises

1. What is the favorite play that you have seen produced? What was it about this production that most captivated you? Comment on the story and the visual impact of the production: set design, central image concept, specific acting, and moments.

2. If you were to note the primary differences between film and theater, without dwelling on the technical aspects, what would you come up with in terms of the different usages of the illusory nature of time, space, character, and action?

3. In plays that you have read or watched, what instances can you find of theatrical conventions? What impact did they have on you as you watched them? How was your imagination challenged in a way that film does not usually manifest?

4. Comment on any framing devices that you have seen used in stage plays that are created by the playwright. How in your estimation did they contribute to the storytelling of your play idea? Note examples not included in the text.

5. What makes the play story idea that you are working on unique to the stage environs? In other words, what have you created visually that film might have a difficult time creating?

6. Why do you love theater?

# Chapter 3

# The Faith-based Writer—
# So Where Is the Faith?

To begin with, I do not think there is such a thing as a "Christian play." There are, hopefully, good stories that have themes and characters, people and ideas that reflect the Christian ethos and belief system. There are, hopefully, good stories that are written by people who profess faith in Jesus. It is something of a misnomer, though convenient, to say, "Christian play"; and I will at times probably succumb to using that label, hoping you will understand what I am talking about and referencing. I say this because by itself the term "Christian play" carries connotations that can immediately initiate warning signs for the prospective reader or audience. These could include: "Are they going to have an altar call?" "Is it a play about biblical stories?" "Am I going to be preached to?" "Well, at least I can be assured that it is going to have a happy ending." "No sex, no foul language, no inappropriate behavior—boring."

As this chapter will explain, the Christian, if she is being true to her belief system, should include at least some of the basic arguments surrounding her faith, because, supposedly, this is the most important thing in her life and what she considers "the Truth." So why does she not do this?

Every writer setting out on the journey of discovering what he wants to write about and how to do that with authenticity, is seeking to find his individualized voice in the stories he wants to tell. American novelist William Faulkner is going to tell a story differently than Russian author Leo Tolstoy or American humorist and fantasy fiction author Thorne Smith. They have found their voices—in their subject matter, style, and approach. Finding one's voice is not simple, and it seems to creep up on you so when it arrives you find yourself thinking: "Ah, that is what I wanted to say all along." In the meantime, you are the victim of a dominant cultural medium that provides an onslaught of stories that are often diametrically opposed to the moral and spiritual presuppositions by which you are trying to live. I know that when I worked for the *Tulane Drama Review* in the mid-1960s, play submissions all sounded like either Samuel Beckett or

Eugène Ionesco. Characters acted out their existence with unrestrained absurdity and broke all the maxims of the well-made play. To this day, though I feel I have found my voice, the subtextual penchant of Harold Pinter remains a constant in my work. So to be totally original is probably not going to happen. Yes, you will echo the voices you most admire that have been successful out there and if you keep writing you will find that your own individual authentic voice will most likely emerge. It just takes time. And that is a journey which can be daunting and keep the novice from staying the course.

Another cause that keeps the youth of today from expressing themselves through the theater is the overwhelming presence of the digital assault—film is the *lingua franca*, or common language of our culture that links individuals and communities in shared realities. Many students who try to learn playwriting have never seen a live professional play production. Movies are where they vicariously experience adventures, romances, and journeys. The fast cut between scenes, limited dialogue, and locations that are diverse and numerous orchestrate the rhythms, focus, and direction of their imaginative lives. How often do I have students writing plays that juxtapose places, actions, and characters in a wild mix of possibilities that the theater would have a very difficult time presenting on stage? I have read many attempts in playwriting that include tanks rolling across the stage; crowds swarming in Central Park; superheroes flashing between buildings; and adjacent scenes moving large landscapes and architectural structures around with glib facility. So the problem is not just introducing the young writer to the conventions and idiosyncrasies of the stage, but hoping they will learn to adjust their imaginations to its limitations, its charm, and its profound communication possibilities.

As a pre-med and English major at Tulane University, I was accepted into the masters of playwriting program, although I had no theater experience. I soon gave up my aspirations as a writer and realized that I needed to learn quite a bit more about how this performance modality worked, so I committed myself to the rigors of acting and directing. What I did learn was what the actor and director bring to the experience of enlivening a play script that I as the writer do not have to include. By beginning to understand what the "beat" was and how it worked for the actor and director, it became easier to write beats that would serve these motivational needs. I also found it useful to study vast areas of dramatic literature to become familiar with the genres as they evolved through the centuries of writing. Immersing myself in the entire intricacies of the art form of theater provided a foundation that was essential for me as a writer to master.

I can imagine a time in the not-too-distant future when younger generations will seek out the communal element of the live theater, where they watch people live on stage working out their problems through story rather than experiencing the near hypnotic effect of virtual reality and the lack of communality inherent in the film form. The empty thrill one feels from the final *Transformer* battle in the 2007 film pales next to the wrenching cosmos-filled act of Oedipus discovering his patricide and incest and the subsequent self-destruction that he brings upon himself in reacting to one of the greatest cultural and societal taboos (*Oedipus Rex*, 429 BC). Or, in that moment when Dr. Faustus, in Christopher Marlowe's *Dr. Faustus* (1592), goes screaming into hell through a trap door in the stage, and the audience is confronted with a man who has lost his soul and refuses to reach out for one last drop of Christ's blood to grab the lifeline of forgiveness and ultimate salvation. And these archetypal actions are happening right in front of us with no intermediaries to separate us from these living personal tragedies. Bruce Long, in his book *The Problem with the Dot*, notes:

> Live theater, especially when infused with the Holy Spirit and Scripture, speaks to the heart with the power to inspire individual change from the inside out. Live theater reminds us of what it means to be human and in community. Live theater reflects and reveals, in equal measure, our relationship to others, and often to God.[1]

Pragmatically, the financial rewards in writing for the theater are somewhat limited. It is difficult to support oneself on the royalties offered in writing for the theater as opposed to the large amounts of money obtained through a film writing contract or becoming a staff writer for a television series. But the fact that a theatrical play can be mounted for just a fraction of the cost of producing a feature film often means that one can see one's work done, performed, and reviewed. One of the reasons that I started a small professional theater company, Saltworks, in Pittsburgh, Pennsylvania, was so that I could direct and produce my own work. Financial remuneration is a consideration, but if you are called to be a writer, I believe it is a secondary consideration. (Chapter 15 offers some observations on writing possibilities for the emerging dramatist.)

Perhaps the writer is haunted by an evangelical tradition that theater, film, and dance put forth material that is morally culpable by the church community. The demand for literalism makes any kind of abstraction (such as dance or surrealism or expressionism) suspect because it is not based on the expression of the cognitive word. I have been the recipient of judgmental criticism for depicting the Witch of Endor on the stage, for having Falstaff drink too much in *Henry IV, Part I* (c. 1597), and for representing God onstage as a smithy in the creation scene of the mystery plays. This can be a daunting situation for the writer when his audience is predisposed to reject many of his conflict-oriented situations as immoral or inappropriate. As a result, the writer may either resort to creating plays that are indistinguishable from the offerings of the dominant culture or decide to quit the creative process all together. We need to avoid an overly optimistic and positive approach when it comes to our writing. Bruce Long, theatrical producer and writer notes:

> with regards to happy endings and the absence of sex, language, and inappropriate behavior, this is a trap developed by the enemy that has been unwittingly embraced by the Church and Christian educators. Christian writers need to free themselves from self-imposed confinement that Christian Film, Christian Theater, Christian anything as being synonymous with family friendly.[2]

He offers the following concerning the state of the art in terms of the faith-based writer:

> The conundrum for many artists of faith then is to create ever-narrowing stories in which the antagonist is just bad enough to create minimal conflict while the protagonist abdicates to Deus ex-Machina resolutions. Consequently, Christian audiences have been conditioned to accept Scripture-brought-to-life stories or poorly told contemporary parables in which salvation solves it all, each rarely escaping the mediocre Christian entertainment niche. This further insulates the audience and forces the creatives into perpetuating evangelistic messaging that has less and less regenerative effect on global culture. We must reverse course, recognize a neglected culture, and tend to it through the power of "a good story well told" that reengages the individual hearts of the global community.[3]

Fears or concerns clank around cacophonously in the Christian writer's mind and may sound like this: "Is my writing inadequate to the task of representing who I am and belong to? Am I creating characters and actions that will offend my orthodox friends? Am I selling out to the world for commercial reasons? Am I selling out to the world and buying into political correctness? Is the world going to laugh at my witness, mock me, accuse me of moral didacticism in the presentation of my faith elements and arguments?" It might, under such circumstances, seem much safer for me to offer up a meal that will be immediately recognizable and consumed with satisfaction by mimicking the popular fare provided by the dominant culture. If I depict a sin action as reprehensible, will I be chastised as psychologically naïve, as intolerant, and as ignorant of the foundations of sin being customarily understood in terms of environmental upbringing, familial pressures, and abuses? The dominant culture will quickly advise you that there is no such thing as original sin, and that, like Freud espouses in his book *Civilization and Its Discontents*, our "polymorphous perversity" is dealt with by accommodating ourselves to the rules and regulations of imposed societal order.[4]

For many decades our culture has been told, by rationalistic philosophers and humanistic psychologists, that sin does not exist. It is alleged to be little more than the mere imaginative concoction of insecure, religious fanatics. Part of finding the want and need to be a writer can be found in developing subjects that you are passionate about and that you feel the culture needs to hear about. A few of these preoccupations and concerns that I have responded to within my own development as a writer are as follows:

- **You cannot do it by yourself**: the discovery that we as humans need the community of our fellows and a personal God to help define and accomplish our purpose in life.

- **We are surrounded by *bona fide* mysteries**; and, how to make the spiritual manifest in awesome terms, rather than just creating draculas or aliens remains a challenge. (Note: "The Mystery Manifesto," observation from an informal meeting at an Arts Within Forum, is located in Appendix 4.)

- **We each have a calling on our lives which foreshadows a sense of destiny**. It is one reason why I appreciate the film *Simon Birch* (1998), which features a theme I have worked on in several of my plays including *Everywoman* (2013) and *Five Cups of Coffee* (2006). Know that we are not just creatures of coincidence.

- **New themes** that I have not fully explored but which are within reach are: "Where is the sense of personal responsibility?"; "Where are our real heroes and what does it do to a culture that has lost them?"; "What are the repercussions of a culture having never been tested as the End-times approach?"

- What are your passions, the questions that plague you, that you feel you desperately need to address through the theatrical medium?

Finally, the aspiring Christian writer might be reluctant to write within the bounds of his belief system because he feels he will be "preaching to the choir." Certainly, as a writer you need to develop the skills of being able to cloak the faith issues you are concerned with communicating in such a way that they are not directed exclusively to the "church crowd" but will have universal appeal. This often means not trying to include the entire salvation message in any one work. My recommendation is to raise questions rather than present pat solutions and give glimpses of redemptive possibilities that point the audience toward hope.

But why not preach to the choir? By preach I do not mean to imply sermonizing with a three-point outline. But preaching, admonishing, and prophesying are exactly what the great prophets, including Christ himself, were doing. Their message was directed to a so-called believing population, the Jewish people in the nation of Israel—in other words, the choir. I personally feel we have reneged on this responsibility. We create a sketch-based approach used as sermon teasers that raise questions, to be sure, but too often they are rehashes of moments already elucidated in Scripture and are valued primarily for their entertainment (keep them from going to sleep in the pews) qualities. Does Christendom not need the challenges that come with confrontation of hypocrisy and calls to action, of examination of their status before God in terms of the state of the seven churches in Revelation?

> *"We, the theatrical artists through our stories, must call the Church to confession and repentance. This is best exemplified through the DC comic* The Watchmen, *in which the recurring slogan, 'Who Watches the Watchmen?' is graffiti-ed everywhere as a warning to hold those in authority accountable for their corruption."* [9]

—Bruce Long

And this brings up the question that echoes in all our physical and spiritual sensibilities: "Have I truly been called to be a writer, much less a writer of plays?" And, of course, in addressing this challenge other questions are raised. Some to be considered are:

- What have been your past affinities for the theater? What creative and spiritual buttons are being pushed when you attend a performance? Do you really want to fill up that space with actors becoming characters that you have written? Do you find yourself wanting to see a live performance more than sitting in a darkened theater watching a movie?

- Can you identify what plays have really moved and excited you, and then take the next step and determine why this is so? This needs to be more than just the appreciation of a good story. There has to be something in terms of how this story is being told that grabs you. This requires a journey to the very heart of your soul in terms of defining your lively engagement in the arts.

- Have you pursued training in the theatrical arts? Do you identify with the struggles of character creation that the actor goes through? Do you perhaps see a story happening in space that you gave birth to in your imagination? Bezalel in Exodus was a trained craftsman in a variety of artistic venues, and obviously was gifted in his artistic acumen. Perhaps he had been called by God to excel as a craftsman without even having a relationship with the Father. God inundated this artist with his Holy Spirit so what he communicated to Bezalel in terms of the creation of the tabernacle, the ark, and surrounding accoutrements, would happen—and happen with excellence. Do you feel that you also have been gifted with the potential of true excellence in some area of theatrical expression?

- Can you say that you have truly heard from our Father in Heaven in terms of a calling to take up writing for the stage? This does not necessarily have to be an audible voice, but could also be answers to prayers, or more than just coincidences in coming up with ideas, with finding yourself drawn to like-minded fellow artists, and responding to the guidance and encouragement offered up by artistic mentors.

- Do you have story ideas within you that have to be told? Are they focused and crying for expression through the filter of your redemptive imagination? In other words, do you want to tell God's story as it may manifest itself in your uniqueness as a child of God?

In summary, then, is there a calling on your heart to write, find your voice, confront your fears through writing and producing your plays knowing that they are addressing a culture that desperately needs to hear and see them? Ultimately, the subjects and stories that you develop, like Jesus's Kingdom parables, will resonate and anchor themselves in the domain you are addressing. The subject matter you deal with is the most important and life-changing material that the creative artist who wants to make a difference can provide. Never hide your light beneath a bushel but take confidence and joy in knowing that this is an apprenticeship for the Kingdom to come. I know that I have learned more from the failures in my playwriting than I have from my victories. It is all a process of learning and preparation—not for making it big here on earth, but for hearing from Him those words that we all so desire to hear: "Well done, good and faithful servant! You have been faithful with a few things; I will put you in charge of many things. Come and share your master's happiness!" (Matt. 25:23, NIV).

And when Jesus sits on his throne in the New Jerusalem, know that your hard work will ultimately be rewarded as you look forward to becoming one of His creative scribes writing for the nations of this earth, and possibly beyond.

## Discussion Questions and Exercises

1. What are the fears that keep you from committing to being a writer? Include viewpoints on personal, cultural, and religious sources for these fears.

2. In developing one's voice as a writer, we are often predisposed toward professional writers who have gone before us. If you have found this to be true, who do you admire as a playwright and why? If they are still living, reach out and make contact and set up an interview.

3. What are your passions, the questions that plague you, that you feel you desperately need to address through the theatrical medium?

4. Look over "The Mystery Manifesto" found in Appendix 4. A key ingredient to consider in writing any faith-based play is the idea that

mystery is what we are living in the middle of. How can we make our audiences aware of any of these mystery principles in our writing?

5. The Old Testament prophets "preached to the choir" in their words to the Jewish believing community. Jesus, in the Book of Revelation, certainly does that as he addresses the seven churches. If you were going to write to and for the church today, what concerns might you raise in terms of messaging theatrical material?

# Chapter 4

# How Then Shall We Write?

"Who am I?" "Where did I come from?" "Why am I here?" "What is wrong with here?" "How can I fix what is wrong with here?" "Where am I going?" and "How do I get there?" These are questions which all of us ask at different times in our lives, or even at different times of any day. The answers to these questions compose the basic foundations of a worldview which will find expression in what we do and speak. As a writer, one is constantly bumping up against the exigencies of characters and plot as they are determined by the search for answers to these questions. Hopefully, any play or film is going to deal with only a fraction of the immensity of the questions presented above, and the best among us will strive to bring fresh and original expression to the answers.

The single worldview that can answer all the above questions positively and consistently is the Christian worldview. For example, the existentialist has no answers to who he is, where he came from, why he is here, what went wrong with here, and he has no idea where he is going. These negatives could be construed as an answer of sorts, but they offer no solutions, the result being that existentialism provides little more than a meaningless quagmire in which one slowly sinks, much as Winnie does in Samuel Beckett's ironically titled play, *Happy Days* (1961). The materialist, on the other hand, professes to have at least a few of the answers: we come from primordial ooze, we create relative value systems to survive in community, and finally we return to the nitrogen cycle. These are answers based on scientific speculations which provide no essential valuation as to the "why" questions of our existence. To formulate a Christian worldview, the creative artist must begin to think in Christian categories: this means being able to define and hold to a world-and-life view oriented in Scripture; it means seeing from a Christian vantage point; it means thinking with the mind of Christ.[1]

The term *worldview* has often been misconstrued to stand for one's culture, with culture being, as noted by Kenneth Myers in *All God's Children and Blue Suede Shoes*:

A dynamic pattern, an ever-changing matrix of objects, artifacts, prejudices, relationships, attitudes, tastes, rituals, habits, colors, sounds, institutions, philosophies, fashions, enthusiasms, fades, myths, and loves which are embodied in individual people, in groups and collectives, and associations of people.[2]

*Culture* is "the secondary environment by which we are formed, it is inescapable," says Henry R. Van Til in *The Calvinistic Concept of Culture*. He continues,

It is totally necessary, and insofar as the writer is concerned it defines the matrix of the material world in which he exists and from which he draws the "context" of so much that he writes. It cannot and should not be ignored, uncritically embraced, or blindly vilified.[3]

Our present multicultural and politically correct society tends to place culture on a pedestal, suggesting that culture is somehow more inclusive than religion. Religion has thus become a mere function of the community or the state, and we can legislate or judicially rule it into our existence or out of it. Sixteenth century pastor and French theologian John Calvin would view this sort of cultural dominance as an apostate worldview, although he would be the last person to turn away from the positive influence that one's surrounding culture can have on the sensible individual. Leland Riken cites Calvin in his book *The Liberated Imagination*:

Whenever we come upon [truth] in secular writers, let that admirable light of truth shining in them teach us that the mind of man, though fallen and perverted from its wholeness, is nevertheless clothed and ornamented with God's excellent gifts. If we regard the Spirit of God as the sole fountain of truth, we shall neither reject the truth itself, nor despise it wherever it shall appear.[4]

So we can and do appreciate the contributions that Harold Pinter has made to the canny play of subtext; Samuel Beckett for finding a meaningful relationship between *form* and *content* in more abstract works; David Mamet's rhythmic and ritualistic use of dialogue; and Sam Shepherd's recognition, treatment, and debunking of American myths.

Where then does this leave the writer who has fully embraced the Christian worldview? If he is indeed an inheritor of a belief structure that exists outside of culture, a belief structure that is above culture and within culture—i.e., in the world but not of the world, see John 15:19—and provides answers to all the epistemological questions of existence, "how then should he write?" The remainder of this chapter will be directed to investigating approaches to this question, especially in terms of how fiction writing can reflect the three basic phenomena of the Christian worldview in terms of Creation, the Fall, and Redemption.

## Creation

After creating the cosmos, the world, and humanity, God found His organic and evolving process to be a good one. By this He not only meant structurally good (sound, balanced, harmonious, aesthetically pleasing) but also morally good, meaning that the relationship between the human being and his Creator was perfect, creative, and meaningful. So right from the beginning, God's creation established the necessity for a symbiosis insofar as form and content are concerned. What does this mean for the writer? It means that he must recognize that we inhabit a moral universe (content) and that the structure (form) of our creation is such that it allows for communication between the Creator and His subjects. There are absolute moral values that are prescribed by Scripture which the writer must be aware of in creating and motivating his characters.

As moral relativism becomes the norm in our culture, postmodern thought and subsequent human behavior discounts moral absolutes. Just about every work of art (even abstract expressionism) implies cultural choices that reflect the artist's viewpoint. In the enclosed world of creative art, a micro-worldview is often implied. Just look at Edvard Munch's painting *The Scream* (1893) or Allen Ginsberg's poem *Howl* (1955). In the film *The Graduate* (1967), all parents are myopically grotesque images of humanity; human relationships are essentially defined within sexual parameters, and the institution of marriage between a man and a woman is mocked. The audience, provided with this highly selective and distorted view of humanity, is given little or no choice but to cheer actor Dustin Hoffman as he runs away with the married bride at the end of the film. The Christian writer has a responsibility to consider the repercussions of the moral choices he provides for his characters.

The concept of judgment at the end of Creation and the implications of humanity's Fall presupposes several content elements which the

Christian-based writer needs to consider. Some of these are personal guilt, the existence of sin as a reality, the freedom of humans to choose evil as opposed to good, and the implications of an ongoing and a final Destiny.

## The Implications of the Reality of Sin

Cultural entertainment has certainly not turned its back on the idea of sin as a culpable choice and, of necessity, a destructive one (Christians have no monopoly over such beliefs.) We see the ill effects that are experienced by Joe Keller for his immoral actions in Arthur Miller's *All My Sons* (1946). By the end of *Godfather III* (1990), we have witnessed the compromising moral choices that have reduced Michael Corleone to an isolated figure. The Lamb's Players's adaptation of *Dracula* (1987) is unique in that it so deftly plumbs the depths of the nature of evil and its warring with good within the human soul and psyche rather than emphasizing the faddish inclination to turn Dracula himself into some sort of romantic hero. The warring against principalities in the form of demon possession, the evil effects of the occult, witchcraft, and other diverse manifestations of evil which are anthropomorphized in werewolves, aliens, and other ghoulish creatures are conscious and unconscious realizations of the spiritual warfare in which human beings are continuously involved.

Frank Peretti's novels and the *Left Behind* (2000) series capitalized on these archetypal fears, though we might wish that they had done so with more artistry and less literalization. In other words, the depiction of the fallen state of humanity has been thoroughly and aptly categorized by secular writers and often trivialized by pulp fiction Christian writers. So where does this leave the serious Christian writer?

Certainly, the pay is good in writing for such amoral sitcoms like *Friends* or *Seinfeld* but at what cost to the basic tenets of your worldview? The Christian writer's commitment should be to portray the fallen state of humanity in terms of a conflict between good and evil, and to depict a context in which the results of choosing evil over good (and vice versa) are aptly expressed. Along the way, she should make sure that sin is not glorified, and, finally, point the way toward the light of possible redemption in the universe created by an awesome, holy, and righteous God. This final caveat is added to deal with other cultural solutions offered up in entertainment fare, including the New Ageism in the film *Grand Canyon* (1991), the psychological insights and breakthroughs in the play *Equus* (1967), and the affirmation of the community and family in the film *On Golden Pond* (1981), in addition to the key themes of friendship, forgiveness, and compassion. There is nothing essentially wrong in films or plays whose final solution is the expression of such themes, to that extent they express the positive God-given attributes of our shared humanity.

The challenge is this: you are a member of God's kingdom who has been blessed with artistic talents, specifically writing. Your desire is to return to God and to the human community the express fruits of your gifts. You realize that there is a great deal of good writing that extols noble values and condemns sinful activity, which is already being written and performed by the apostate culture around you. Why then do you choose to replicate these works when you have been provided with a precious insight into the workings of God in creation through His Son and the Holy Spirit? The rub comes when you ask the question: how can I do this without seeming to preach, to proselytize, or to revert to bumper sticker theology in the expression of my work? How can I do this without cheapening or trivializing the mysterious and awesome insights into the ineffable that God has made uniquely mine? One of the ways is through realizing a sense of destiny.

## Destiny

*"Religious faith is necessary to understand human destiny. And man in his faith is covenantally related to a Being that is transcendent, and, because of this covenantal relationship, which constitutes true religion, man has an eternal destiny, which transcends culture."*[5]

To write with a sense of destiny recognizes that there is a purpose outside of oneself that is guiding, interacting, and even manufacturing the course of a character's action. John Irving realizes this in his novel *A Prayer for Owen Meany* (1989) and Todd Stein articulates this same sense in his film *2:22* (2017)—what if there is no such thing as a coincidence? What if all these little things in our lives have meaning? Frederick Buechner deepens our awareness of this realization when he writes:

The question is not whether the things that happen to you are chance things or God's things because, of course, they are both at once. There is no chance thing through which God cannot speak—even the walk from the house to the garage that you have walked ten thousand times before, even the moments when you cannot believe there is a God who speaks at all anywhere. God speaks, I believe, and the words are incarnate in the flesh and blood of ourselves and of our own footsore and sacred journeys.[6]

A character or an audience's burgeoning awareness of this phenomenon of destiny is at the heart of the existential religious experience, even though it does not have to be couched in religious terms. The paradox is that all of this is expressed within the knowledge that we are creatures imbued with *free will*—that is, with the capability of resisting and denying the reality of this destiny phenomenon in our journey. What a rich field to explore in terms of the meaning of life! I personally think that if we could imbue our audiences with an evolving sense that there is more to our experience than mere happenstance, and that someone out there has a personal plan for our lives that supersedes environment and heredity, then we will have accomplished something lasting and significant in communicating an awareness of what life and afterlife are all about.

## Choices

> *"I call heaven and earth as witnesses today against you, that I have set before you life and death, blessing and cursing; therefore, choose life, that both you and your descendants may live; that you may love the Lord your God, that you may obey His voice, and that you may cling to Him, for He is your life and the length of your days."* (Deut. 30:19–20, NKJV)

The choices that you offer to your characters become essential in defining their worldview. And the various plot points that you create in your story should progressively complicate your protagonist's life in terms of the moral and value systems that they accept or reject. The nature of these choices will establish a worldview context for your protagonists and antagonists that will be recognizable as well as truthful to your audience.

## Structure

One of the measures of a play's artistic authenticity can be determined through examining the relationship between form and content in the story that is being unfolded. The ritualistic formalism of Aeschylus' *Agamemnon* (458 BC) is congruent with the onstage pageantry and offstage killing of a king in the highest places. The wagons which moved through European towns and presented ongoing enactments of the biblical narrative during medieval times, and which were built by the guilds and sponsored by the church, offered a structural equivalency to the idea of the "Great Chain of Being" which was reflective of the cosmological worldview of the time.

The revolutionary Russian filmmaker, Sergei Eisenstein, strove to find a structural model (conflict montage) that would be the best vehicle to express the Marxist dialectic. Samuel Beckett created desolate wastelands to portray the shriveled characters and the absurdity of life which he portrays in his existential dramas. Bertolt Brecht created a theater of fragmented scenery supplemented by various musical and media devices that were devised to alienate his audience from empathizing with his characters so that his socialist message could be more strongly communicated. Each author and director devised what they felt would be the ideal form elements to carry their philosophical worldview or content preoccupations.

Is there then an ideal structure for playwriting that would best contain the Christian worldview? Of course not. Our cosmology is too all-inclusive to be contained in a single structural reality. Scripture itself contains songs, poetry, epic, parable and dramatic narrative, flashbacks, flashforwards, and a final chapter which is dreamlike and charged with symbolism. God has provided a host of paradigms which can free you as a writer from being restricted to a comfortable domestic realism reflective of the sitcom waste which surrounds us. Why not take advantage of this freedom? For example, Lucia Frangione's play *Espresso* (2004) offers up a two hander in which each actor plays multiple characters, transitions from place to place with the simple manipulation of a prop or costume piece. It moves from reality to abstraction, from exterior to interior voices, in a stripped-down theatrical context, all telling the story of a woman's intense psychological struggle within herself, her family, and with her God.

The use of time is usually considered to be a structural element, but in the hands of such writers as Samuel Beckett and Harold Pinter, it also assumes a content mantle. Gogo and Didi are depicted in *Waiting for Godot* (1952) as existing in a world where day arbitrarily changes to night and in which there is no concrete sense of history being played out in the context of a diminishing sense of future possibility. The realm of potential action has been reduced to the here and now, to the scrambling after appetite.

In the Bible we are presented with a different image of time. The fullness of the biblical narrative has a definite beginning-middle-end to it so far as the history of this earth is concerned. We are notably affected by the sins of our fathers going back generations, and we have definitive promises to look forward to in the future. What does this tell us about how we should write? Should all plays congruent with a Christian worldview be sequential narratives? Christ was, is, and will be, and if we take this para- doxical axiom and combine it with the multifarious literary paradigms evidenced in Scripture, we find ourselves able to write with unshackled structural autonomy.

Perhaps one of the delights as well as one of the burdens of being a writer and a believer is the realization that God has provided a way out of the fallenness of this world. Christ is at the heart of this redemptive act, and to deny the efficacy of what He accomplished on the cross through the reality of his resurrection is to deny the very essence of our world- view. This earth-shattering resurrection action is a mystery; it bridges the material and spiritual worlds; it implies the working presence of the Holy Spirit within and without. The burden mentioned above becomes this: how do we present images, reflections, and echoes of this reality in our dramatic work without compromising the awe, wonder, fear, and majesty that it demands? One way is through how we deal with the concept of character change.

## Character Change

A common phrase that emerges from play and film writing texts is that "characters don't change." We are what we are, and all our psychologi- cal tendencies are formed by the age of five. We do not change, we merely realize potentialities, fears, and traits that have always been buried within us. There is some truth here, but the Christian worldview offers a very dif- ferent concept of change in which we "are being transformed into his image with ever-increasing glory, which comes from the Lord, who is the Spirit" (2 Cor. 3:18, NIV). This sort of transformational impetus comes from with- out and is directly tied to our faith stance and to the sanctified walk that we experience after salvation. How to depict this reality is one of the great challenges of the Christian writer.

Scripture tells us that Matthew dropped his tax collecting duties and followed Jesus, but we are not invited in to the psychological and spiritual pressures that brought about this radical change in his life. But his actions tell us that something startling happened. A more complete rendition of change is provided through the depiction of Zacchaeus, another tax col- lector (see Luke 19:1–10). In his overwhelming desire to see Jesus, he runs down the street and climbs a tree, which compromises his social and occupational station in life. He agrees to invite Jesus into his house, inviting all of his so-called sinner friends to come along. The next morning, he restores what he has stolen from people "four times the amount" (19:8, NIV).

The important element of writing that we can learn here is that Scripture does not provide us with a long monologue in which Zacchaeus tells us how he was saved by Jesus; instead, it demonstrates through a series of key actions the state of his mind and his ultimate turn around. Ebenezer Scrooge in Charles Dickens's novella *A Christmas Carol* (1843) does not stop to give us a treatise about how the visiting spirits changed his life; rather, he throws open the window to his cold apartment and buys a goose and Christmas presents for the Cratchits and for his family. In *Paper Wings* (1995), we watch Jamie's faith foundation grow and replace the emotional up and down dynamics which she evidenced in Act One through a series of actions that speak to her new life in Christ. We know and ultimately believe a person not by their words but by their actions.

## Christlikeness

Jesus's impact on all of history—including religious mythical paradigms expressed in both Jewish and gentile cultures before His coming in the flesh—reverberates through literary, theatrical, and filmic presentations. The image of Christ portrayed through his attributes as a model of the hero is prevalent and can represent a way of depicting aspects of our worldview in other-than-biblical modalities. Christ as the scapegoat is seen in the sacrificial lamb of Jewish atonement rites, but also in Agamemnon's *Prometheus Bound* (479 BC), Sophocles' *Oedipus Rex* (429 BC), William Shakespeare's *Richard II* (1597), Edmond Rostand's *Cyrano de Bergerac* (1897), and in such films as *The Mission* (1986) and *In America* (2002). The novels of Wendall Berry in their portrayal of the long-suffering citizens of Port Williams, Kentucky, who strive after goodness and eternal values, reflect many aspects of the Christ person and message as does the main character of *Mr. Ives' Christmas* (1995) by Oscar Hijuelos. And Christ-like innocence brings ultimate destruction to Prince Mishkin in Fyodor Dostoyevsky's *The Idiot* (1869). The Duke's forgiveness at the end of *Measure for Measure* (1604), Francis' transformation into a saint/man united with the natural elements in Franco Zeffirelli's *Brother Sun, Sister Moon* (1972), and even Joan's striving to fulfill and make complete God's destiny for herself and those around her in *Joan of Arcadia* (2003–2005), are all Christlike impulses manifest in story and character, the emulation of which deserves further exploration by the sensitive Christian writer.

## The Objective Correlative

Poet Gerald Manley Hopkins writes: "The world is charged with the grandeur of God."[7] Writer and critic T. S. Eliot corroborates this view in his concept of the "objective correlative," which essentially says that matter itself can be imbued with anthropomorphic attributes, and that it can reflect both the spiritual and the emotional state of characters in literary fiction.[8] Thus, when the moral balance of both Thebes (*Oedipus Rex*) and Denmark (*Hamlet*, c. 1600) is upset, this is reflected through plagues and rottenness which assault the physical environments. Lear's madness in *King Lear* (c. 1606) is mirrored in the tempestuous storm on the heath; the suffocating sexuality and mendaciousness of Christopher Hampton's *Les Liaisons Dangereuses* (1988) is realized through claustrophobic boudoirs, screens, fans, and cumbersome make-up.

In other words, the physical world reflects the moral state of the characters. That nations and individuals are or will be punished for their moral turpitude through plagues, droughts, invasions, earthquakes, and financial ruin is consistent with biblical revelation. The writer is obligated to inculcate this principle in his work to take advantage of the dynamic power of living symbols which can reflect moral values as well as states of mind in the lives and actions of his characters. The richness that follows is often the difference between talking about or literalizing values as opposed to subjectively establishing them through symbolic objects and actions.

> *"For since the creation of the world God's invisible qualities—his eternal power and divine nature—have been clearly seen, being understood from what has been made, so that people are without excuse."*
>
> Rom. 1:20 (NIV)

We hear Christians justifying their writing by using such terms as "redemptive" or "transformational." If the play has a redemptive message, it is automatically "Christian." But what often is implied is that it has a happy ending, that good wins out over evil, that marriage and community are restored, and that it represents safe family values. Certainly, there is nothing wrong with creating stories that reflect aspects of the Christian ethos, but again it should be emphasized that the above values are being regularly produced on television and film projects within the dominant culture. To write redemptively stands for far more than fuzzy and warm happy endings or feel-good sentiments that allow us to leave the theater whistling those feel-good moral tunes that played over our sensibilities for two hours. True redemption is the result of a transformational process which has as its origin the radical intrusion of the saving grace of God through his Son, Jesus Christ into our fallen world. From this standpoint, the purpose of redemption is much like the purpose of art itself: to jolt us out of our material complacency; to make us see the world through new lenses; and to give new purpose and insight and meaning into our mundane lives.

As Christians, the Holy Spirit dwells within each one of us. We are all walking miracles. The ineffable resides within. That is remarkable and shattering in its scope. And along with it comes a great responsibility to share with the world the repercussions of this phenomenon of God-within. Daily we are aware that we exist on the cusp of a spiritual reality that is a vast mystery. We commune with a living and personal God, we are aware of warring with principalities, and we live literally on our toes in anticipation of this God interacting and intervening in our lives. This is the most precarious, the most challenging, and the most demanding walk that any human being can experience. That it should be the motivation for our creative impetus, in some form or other, is not at all unbecoming. How to articulate this mystery without sentimentality, without purposeful sensationalism, or a deadening proselytizing voice is the challenge (For more on the concept of mystery refer to Appendix 4.)

## Transcendence and Incarnation

Christ provides us with the model. He was God made incarnate in the material world as a man, as flesh and blood. He preached the Kingdom through parable and paradox. His actions healed, soothed, outraged, and amazed the world. He became the perfect blending of form and content. At the same time, he transcended this life. Angels announced his coming. He expunged demons, was transfigured, raised the dead with the command of his voice, and ultimately defeated death itself, returning in a new bodily form that brought together the noumenal and phenomenal.

The dynamic infusion of God in the world is the energy that the Christian writer has to catch, harness, and reproduce in diverse ways: God in flesh, God in material reality, God wanting to break out of this material world and flash out light to a world still muddled in darkness. The Christian writer must make the "impossible" possible in his work by reflecting, echoing, shadowing, and even manifesting the walking miracles we are as human beings. Oftentimes it is just a moment, like at the end of Lucia Frangione's *Espresso*, an angel lifts his broken but transformed partner and carries her about the stage to the sound of eagle's wings. Or it is like the moment where the pope kneels and kisses the dirty feet of Friar Lawrence in *Brother Sun, Sister Moon*. In *Five Cups of Coffee* (2006), a man obsessed with the turnings of time stands at the rusted gates of the Garden of Eden and decides to return to real time to become a parent and a partner in a way that he had never before. In *In America*, a man dies and a baby lives. In Robert Bresson's *Diary of a Country Priest* (1951), a woman kneels and receives the Holy Spirit, but this is shown only through light and the empty vicarious spying of an apostate priest. The list goes on.

When the transcendent springs from the actions and symbols of our natural environment, it has a particular evocative power. And for the audience it becomes immediately identifiable and possible. Flannery O'Connor throws down the gauntlet: "As grace and nature have been separated, so imagination and reason have been separated, and this always means an end to art."[9]

Are we capable of infusing our fictional environments and the characters and stories that we create with a sense of destiny, with universal moral dictums, with Christ-like imagery and actions, with gestures and words which signify the wonder and awesome presence of our Lord in both mundane and life changing moments? Are we up to the challenge of bringing a new trans-Genesis to our fallen culture through what we write?

## Discussion Questions and Exercises

1. This chapter includes several elements that the faith-based writer might consider when developing an aesthetic as a storyteller. These include choice, destiny, the idea and meaning of sin, transcendence, and more. What element(s) might you add to this list that might be considered appropriate and even a necessary part of the author's

approach to story? You are concerned here with what makes a story good in a faith context rather than the personal disciplines that the writer might use in approaching and completing the story.

2. Have you ever read or seen a story on the stage or screen that you felt violated you as a Christian? Why was this? What did you learn from this encounter?

3. What stage play or film has changed your life? Can you describe how and why this happened? What have been the consequences of this personal and aesthetic experience?

4. Do you feel called to being a writer? If so, how did this happen? What sort of writing challenge do you feel you need to develop to fulfill this calling?

# Chapter 5

# Inspiration

*"I pray that the eyes of your heart may be enlightened in order that you may know the hope to which he has called you."*
*(Eph. 1:18, NIV)*

HOW OFTEN HAVE I HEARD, "But Gil, I do not have any stories to tell" when I ask my students to come up with ideas for feature films or plays? I can sit down with anyone and within half an hour of talking to them about their heritages, their studies, their fears, their passions, and their desires come up with possible ways of couching these emotions and remembrances into a story mode.

What about your childhood? What do you keep going back to? For me it is my relationship with my father, who keeps appearing in my plays in various disguised manifestations. He was a brilliant artist and accomplished pianist who played totally by ear. When I asked my father at the age of twelve if I could be an artist like him, he drew a three-dimensional airplane and told me to draw it myself without tracing. For three days I sweated over trying to emulate his WW2 sketch of a P-51 Mustang fighter banking into a dive and failed miserably. He told me I would never be a painter. He was right.

I ended up directing and writing, two artistic disciplines for which he had no inclination. In other words, I have always felt competitive with my father, and somehow think that I have come up a bit short of accomplishing what he has. Interestingly, I realized that I had some sort of artistic inclination in high school when I excelled at geometry, while efforts at algebra or calculus were near disasters. I could see those triangles and trapezoids moving three dimensionally in space. Later, as a director, I exploited this talent by moving actors and props within the theater space to tell stories; and often hints of my relationship with my father would manage to make at least a cameo appearance. So explore your childhood to find your story: neighborhood wars, sibling rivalries, that first musical comedy you saw, that first kiss, or running away from home. The list goes on.

If you are a metaphor-maker, then start training yourself in the art of associational thinking. Scribble down words and phrases that are the beginnings of stories. You are sitting in a traffic jam. What do those people, those trees, remind you of? They say a dog owner resembles their pet. What is the story there? Hey, wait! What is that mousy looking fellow doing with a pit bull?

What do you read? Watch? What effect do these encounters with the work of other creative artists have on you? I remember as an English major my sophomore year in college when suddenly two things happened: first, I read William Faulkner's *As I Lay Dying* (1930), and second, I saw Ingmar Bergman's *The Seventh Seal* (1957). Both introduced me to dynamic worlds of symbolism, and for the first time the associational power of metaphor-making clicked. I realized that the journey of transporting a mother's dead body became the vehicle for the arguments for and against the very idea of existence. In Bergman's film, a disillusioned knight plays chess with Death to prolong his life in plague-afflicted Europe as he returns from the crusades. The metaphysics of life and death are toyed with, but it is all just a game that in the end we all lose. Similar approaches to ultimate questions played out in two entirely different times and environments.

Look at the death, birth, wedding, divorce, and other ritual cycles in our lives. These are places to start—and to end—in terms of forming stories that reflect your ethos but can be related to by virtually every human being. A year after my *The Seventh Seal* experience I saw a production of Harold Pinter's *The Birthday Party* (1958). I heard and saw subtext played verbally and physically like I had never heard and seen before. I actually stood up in the theater I was so amazed at what could be accomplished during a pause that the person behind me told me to sit down.

> *"There is no greater agony than bearing an untold story inside you."*[1]
>
> —Zora Neale Hurston

By choosing to be an artist, you are not only searching for your story, but how you can share what is worth sharing. This sharing is your creative spill, what goes out to the world, and how it throws light on how to live or how not to live. The search for the root of possible story elements should be relentless as you pursue people and places. Notebooks should be overflowing with phrases, ideas, doodles, and quotes that say something to you. Record it or you will lose it.

Every year my wife and I travel to England to rent a cottage and walk the cliffs of Cornwall. Sometimes we go with another couple. Recently, it was with Sean and Catherine Gaffney, a professional writer and actress in the theater. We established a challenge which was comprised of sharing our experiences, seeing stone circles, or talking with a fisherman for the purposes of showing how they could be framed into possible stories. In the past, I explored Glastonbury in Somerset, a gathering place of modern-day Druids who worship at the giant oak trees in Selwood Forest, and the place where King Arthur is supposed to one day return. We have walked the paths that C. S. Lewis trod with J. R. R. Tolkien in Devon and Cornwall and explored the ancient tin mines filmed in the *Poldark* (2015) BBC series.

A smattering of people on our walks whom we stopped and shared with include the following: a stone mason who rebuilds ancient stone walls and wishes he had Italian roots; the CEO of a gold mining company in Tanzania who would not tell us the name of his company; a retired truck driver who walks the coast of Cornwall by himself in search of the perfect fish and chip establishment; a photographer who keeps moving to smaller and smaller fishing villages to avoid the high-class restaurateurs as they move into town; and a former record collector, now gardener, who imports rare plants from New Zealand because he is convinced that he is going to have the last repository of rare plants from that area in the world. Did you know that Joseph of Arimathea was the uncle of Jesus and took him to visit his tin mines in Southwest England when he was a teenager? Or so the myth goes. We tracked down the mines and the songs that were the source of this tale. A short story/poem I wrote the summer of 2017, *Andy and Reggie*, records an actual set of encounters that happened in St. Ives over a three-year period:

*ANDY AND REGGIE*

St. Ives, a carbuncle on Cornwall's boot,
Where, walking the commercial drag,
The smell of lamb Pasties,
Fudge slathered with Cornish clotted cream,
Galleries with an endless parade of seascapes,
The half-moon harbor, tide out, boats cantered,
We happened by a small, old, Methodist Church.

Wedding music wafted onto Fore Street.
Inside the groom, tuxedo, bent over,
Was being married to a flaxen haired beauty,
Striking in her white dress and lace.

The bridegroom levered by two of his male entourage,
Could hardly say, "I do."
They sat at a table, as if agreeing to a contract,
The bride had no one to throw the flowers to.
A song, then it was over, no kiss exchanged.
And as I wondered how and why,
Beauty and the broken beast made their way,
Toward the store front entrance to the chapel.

In the narrow-cobbled street outside sat the limousine,
Motor running, tourists gliding by on either side.
Reggie and Andy, for that was their names,
Emerged. No rice.
Reggie, in the later grip of muscular dystrophy
Was half carried to the front seat,
Where he lolled while
Andy sat in the back.

Scenarios played themselves out in my writer's head,
So, I approached with some trepidation
A huge-bristled Scotsman kilted to the brim,
Who stood crying, and in between sobs and the rush of air,
Related a narrative of sorts. . .

"Been living together. . . they used to watch my bairns.
Fishing trips. . . sweetest man. . . the two of them,
Living as one, not married, oh no,
But one still daft aboot the other,
When he comes down with the limb girdled curse.

So's things worsen,
And he gets bit by what's drivin'
The brethren in there,
Never had time for it myself.
Plus, there was matters of money,
Gettin' married so the State don't
Scarf up the leavin's."
I think the worse: Marriage of convenience,
Separate vacations; a lover on the side.
Patience running thin.
How long can this last?

# INSPIRATION

Two years later we return to St. Ives,
Older, slower, cliff wary, joint weary,
And on the spur, Sunday morn,
We make our way into Fore Street Methodist
 As the Congregation Sings,
"Nearer My God to Thee."

On the right, across the aisle,
Sit Andy and Reggie.
Sit isn't an apt description,
For a quiet but continuous frenzy ensues.

As his hands become gnarled, she soothes them out,
She turns his head, lifts his hands in a mute praise,
And with a cup gathers saliva.
She catches me watching,
Her eyes reading, "steady on" no desperation,
No pleas for justice or put-uponness,
Just a resignation to thirty second ministrations
That will never end until. . .

During the sermon they left the service,
Doing a strange broken dance as she walks
Backwards holding his hands,
Opening doors and dancing thru.
A pause, then back again to sit,
But the dance will never end.

The Minister was preaching from the Gospel of John,
Of a time before the Messiah's death,
When he knelt and washed his disciples' feet.
"I have set you an example, that you should do as I have done for you."
And across the aisle it was being done.
As hands were smoothed,
Neck gently rubbed; arms lifted for the release of breath.
Communion would round out the service.
Andy broke off a piece of bread,
And held the small plastic cup of juice,
Serving her mate, the body and the blood,
A liturgy in and unto itself,
As He would have us do for one another.

I became more aware then of the woman at my side,
Fifty years my companion,
And wondered if I too would kneel and serve,
And do a dance with her, one breath,
Together, until the temporal exigencies,
The husks that awkwardly encapsulate our Spirits,
Turn to dust and swirl towards the light eternal.

So, thank you Andy and Reggie,
For the Word become flesh
For the reminder that a tremor
Or a breath from the one we love,
Are worthy of our lasting attention,
And that you allowed us to catch a brief glimpse of
The Christ within.[2]

So know this: you remain the greatest repository of story resources as you apply your story generating imagination to your day-by-day experiences, and as you contemplate your own story elements. Ask yourself what do you fear? And why? What do you hate and why? What do you love and why? What is the story there? What are the connections? I have a fear of failure and therefore end up challenging myself with projects where I might fail so I can take on this compromised area of my personality. Another fear is that I will produce bad, or worse, mediocre art, and that I will not know it, or I will think it is good. Or what if I stopped living on the edge of "What If's" in my life?

A theme I find that I keep coming back to in my life and writing is, "you cannot do it by yourself." Perhaps that is one of the reasons that I became a believer in Christ, because of the acknowledgment that I need Him on a continuing basis, and it is when I start searching on my own that I get in real trouble.

> *"The work is too heavy for you;*
> *you cannot handle it alone."*
>
> Ex. 18:18 (NIV)

## What Is Your Passion?

American novelist F. Scott Fitzgerald observes: "You don't write because you want to say something; you write because you've got to say something."[3]

I believe that writers must be passionate about this world. Oftentimes it might be one theme. I care about the death of children; I care about the plague of loneliness; I care about what is happening to the family today; I care about personal and social freedoms. As a Christian, I care about cultivating the mystery of my faith; I care about communicating that we cannot do it by ourselves, that we need God in our life; I care about my unsaved friends; I care about (fill-in-the-blank).

If you really care about something, care enough to put it in a good story, with characters who are flawed but passionate. And include a final message that is earned through truthful actions enacted by truthful characters, saying things that are true to themselves, not just to you as a writer/ Christian. This is a creative bonus.

If you are writing but not passionate about what you are writing, then you have sold out commercially. Or you are lying to yourself. Or you have settled for second best. If this is true, you can still be technically proficient, but the passion of your heart will not be communicated to others.

"But Gil, I am passionate about Jesus Christ." Yes. So am I. But perhaps you want to write about a character who is passionate about making money, and we see the destitute state of his life without Christ. Or perhaps you want to write about a man who is a sinner but who is passionately searching for something more, and perhaps his search will point others to look for God. Or perhaps you want to write about a person who finds just a flicker of God's light in someone else.

Too often, our passion is so overwhelming that we want to tell the entire story of salvation, sanctification, death, and eternal life all in one play. But perhaps it would be a more effective story if we found other ways to express this passion. So do not let your passion for Christ be expressed through bumper sticker theology and language. Do not let your characters be perfect after their salvation, and do not make the spiritual choices easy for your characters. Finally, do not be afraid to depict the fallen side of life. For how can we know redemption if we do not know fallenness? Do not make the passion for your faith into a formula.

Let your passion for Christ and for writing be oriented toward a passion of mastering your craft as much as it is toward communicating the salvation message. Let your passion take you on a ride into areas that you have never investigated before. Challenge your audiences with new forms and new ideas. Put your new wine into new wineskins.

## *"The desire to write grows with writing."*[4]

### —Erasmus

Back in the days when I would jog, if I did not exercise, I would feel angry and be short-tempered. I had trouble sleeping at night and felt that something was missing. You have probably felt the same way yourself, and, if not, known someone else who has. The same goes for writing. If you are working on a piece and you stop writing for a week, returning to it is like returning to a distant relative. You may ask, "did I write that?"

Once you get started in writing daily, you look forward to it. If a doctor's appointment or having the car inspected takes up your normal writing time, you feel a bit disenfranchised for that day. Write so it becomes a ritual. Write so that if you do not do it, then it is like missing a meal or a heartbeat. I love to write. Some people dread it, but do it anyway, which is a hate-love relationship that I am glad I am not in.

I think we find the same thing goes with our spiritual walks. If we are into daily prayer, Bible study, and meditation, we find that God's word speaks to us in an easier manner than if we are grabbing a time with the Lord in between business deals or other engagements. We grow in our relationship with the Lord in proportion to the quality time that we spend with him. As a writer, we are constantly challenging ourselves to come up with a better, more effective beat or scene. We work best when we are not playing catch up. The same goes for our spiritual walk. If we want it to become more than a walk, but a jog or even a run, then we must be in shape. We must have done our preparation otherwise we end up staying the same.

I can remember as a runner that after so many miles at a certain pace those endorphins kick in and you really get a second wind, a sort of physical high, and you do not ever want to stop. Writing can be the same way: when you are doing it, your right brain kicks in, your sense of time goes out the window, and you are transported into the world of your own creation. Can you say the same thing about your spiritual life? Try meditating on Jesus. After a while, God begins to speak. Discipline gives you the freedom to create with abandon and still have it be good.

*"I shall live badly if I do not write, and*
*I shall write badly if I do not live."*[5]

—Francois Sagan

## Story is Where You Are, and Where You Go

There is no doubt about it: you must have experienced life to write truthfully about it. If not, then you will be rehashing other people's experiences, or doing a new turn on an old story idea. This is called second-hand writing. If you are going to write a science fiction play then you need to know the science and the fiction.

One common experience of writing students is that they want to write what they have seen on film. So we get another horror show or another *Bourne Identity* (2002) spinoff. Then what can we account of as first-hand experience?

- Our childhood
- Our travels
- Our work
- Relationships
- Our passions
- Our inner thoughts and emotions

We cannot write about something we do not know. Kurt Luedtke studied coffee plantations for years before he wrote about them in the film *Out of Africa* (1985). The film *Alien* (1996) has a truck stop reality to it. They are hauling goods. Someone who wrote that film knew a lot about trucks. If we do not have the experience, we make the experience. You do this as a writer so that you can develop your own voice and can contribute something that is not a rehash of the work of other writers before you.

Like the man of faith, the artist conceives, then experiences, then reorders the experience so that it becomes art. If this translation of experience to the written word is truthful and profound and artful, then it will transfer that experience to the reader.

British writer Peter Terson was a games teacher when he was discovered as a writer by Peter Cheeseman, artistic director of the Victoria Theater in Stoke on Trent, England. Periodically, he would leave his job and his family and find work someplace else. Often, this would result in a new play, many of which ended up on the West End or at regional professional theaters. Engage where you are and venture to new places to stir the story initiatives that are waiting to find expression. A few examples from my own writing are included below.

To begin, my play *Paper Wings* (1995) was based on what I experienced in my own home as my mother became a Christian and my father strenuously resisted it. Another script, *For Better, For Worse* (1989), was based on the story surrounding my minister running away with my best friend's wife. Trips to Ireland prepared me for *Brendan's Journey* (1997) and walking the South Downs from Winchester to Canterbury on the Pilgrim's Way provided the impetus for a special adaptation of Geoffrey Chaucer's *The Canterbury Tales* (2001).

Additionally, my wife, our children, and I would travel to York and Chester, England to view modern resurrected productions of the mystery plays which resulted in my own musical adaptation of these medieval classics. I wrote and directed *Steel/City* (1976), a musical documentary, while at the University of Pittsburgh in one of the urban areas where the steel industry was in the last gasps of its once great industrial tradition. I spent a year traveling up and down the Mon Valley interviewing retired steel workers and their wives, utilizing their stories as a template for the authenticity of the stage play. In another instance, a visit to Onancock, Virginia, became the geographical source for a filmscript titled *Skipjack* (2015), the story of how a waterman's family is torn apart when one of them acquires the gift of healing. *Pittsburgh Ho!* (1995) toured the steel town schools, a participatory play featuring the mythic characters who have regional associations such as Joe Magerac, born in a steel crucible; Mike Fink, the riverboat man; and Johnny Appleseed, who passed through on his way to the Midwest. The Pittsburgh environments also served as the location for a feature film titled *Miracle Mile* (2006).

Some practical advice for story idea expansion includes the following:

- Make sure you have both an intellectual and emotional connection with what you want to say. How passionately do you feel the need to write a story on your idea? And how passionately do you identify with possible characters—can you laugh and weep with them?

- Understand your own stumbling blocks that might complicate your idea presentation. What are the prejudices that might creep in? What are you afraid of saying because of friends or relatives? Some critics suggests that you should not write anything that you would not want Jesus to read. What does that mean to you?

- Be a persistent student of characters and events. Do you carry a notebook with you? Do you find yourself leaning in to overhear conversations? Do you make up plays or scenes or moments in your mind on a continual basis, and then do you write them down? Do you also write down snippets of dialogue you might read or see in the media? Developing as a playwright is a lifelong commitment. Start early and keep records; you will thank yourself repeatedly.

- Write what you know. This means that you cannot just observe but must also explore the positive and negative contingencies of life. You must challenge yourself to meet new people and develop a curiosity that will compel you to explore avenues you never thought navigable before. The joy of being a writer is that you are a "Renaissance person": you cannot wait to figure out how something works, and what it does to those who are doing it. But this knowledge base should also include your imagination. You might not be familiar with a unicorn, but you can imagine this half-horse being, and you can put this creature in a fantasy setting that is a compilation of what you have read, seen in the movies, and dreamt about. So what you know becomes an extension of factual real people and incidents and your imaginative take on these realities.

- Constantly expose yourself to all sorts of visual and aural creations: music, media, zoos, museums, vacation spots, dreams, and visions. Are you fascinated with the little things, like the way grandpa rides around in his wheelchair? Or the way your sister wants to feed all the wildlife she encounters? Or what people are hiding and why?

It has often been said of artists that they have one thing to say. There is some truth in this. But having one thing to say by itself can be a major contribution, and a good artist will find many ways to say it. Often, what this artist has to say is intrinsic to who he is and what is weighing on his heart. Have you found this to be true? Do you keep returning to a single theme and reoccurring characters? There is a lifetime of writing in exploring a theme that reflects your passionate engagement with who you are and what you want to say to the world.

## Discussion Questions and Exercises

1. The Bible is a first-rate inspirational source for the believing artist. What stories, characters, and actions have most inspired you to want to write about them? Make a list. Let's say you chose the story of Hannah and Samuel. How would you expand on what is already provided? What conversations do you imagine going on between Hannah and her husband, or between Samuel, Hannah, and God? Why did you pick the moment or story that you did? If the story speaks to you, what is it saying?

2. If you were going to write a play about a Christian personality who made an impact on society, who would you select? Why this character? What do you most identify with concerning his or her life story?

3. In your encounters with the culture around you, what feeds you the most from the standpoint of ideas for possible plays? What about other plays you have been influenced by? Movies? Television shows? Novels and newspapers? Do you find some patterns of character and thematic interest evolving here?

4. List the milestone moments in your life up to the present. Ten would be sufficient. These should be equivalent to possible plot point moments when things changed, when you were emotionally challenged, when you had some sort of breakthrough personally. Explore a couple of them in terms of time, place, and small/major actions that involve conflict. What can you cull from these moments that would serve possible stories you are in the process of thinking about or creating?

5. Who is the most idiosyncratic character you have ever known? Describe her in terms of her actions, worldviews, dress, and unique characteristics.

6. Write down what you feel God is laying on your heart in terms of what He might be calling you to write about, or at least consider. Take one or two of these callings and note what story aspects you are coming up with or can imagine coming up with in terms of making them an organic part of a story matrix.

7. You remain the greatest repository of story resources as you apply

your story-generating imagination to your daily experiences and contemplate your own story elements. Ask yourself what you fear and why? What you hate and why? What you love and why? What is the story there? What are the connections? Write them down. Do not avoid but embrace them. They are a part of you, so welcome them as an aspect of self-expression in your writing.

# PART TWO

# Chapter 6

# Writing the Play

THE CHAPTERS BEGINNING IN PART TWO feature the less esoteric and the more practical elements involved in writing for the theater. Theater has been defined as a performance with drama as its literary corollary. But it is also important that the writer understands the practical exigencies of how theater works. Do you have an image in your head of actors moving around in a limited space? Do you see them using props, eating, smoking, entering, and exiting? Do you realize that what you envision on the stage as happening must be constructed, moved, painted, and then torn down? "You mean that I cannot go where I want and do whatever comes to mind?" Certainly, you can. No limitations. But rather than falling back on the escape clause, "I write it, let the director figure out how to make it happen," developing an image for the workable conventions that allow you to cavort over continents and create large crowds with a cast of six can be of utmost importance. Shakespeare, for example, moves through environments with great fluidity. However, he knows he is writing for an open stage that has an absolute minimum of theatrical devices and set pieces, and that the language itself and the use of an important prop can tell the story and clue the audience into the "where" and "when" questions that might crop up in their minds. George Bernard Shaw, in his opening stage directions for *Arms and the Man* (1894) reads as follows:

ACT I

Night. A lady's bedchamber in Bulgaria, in a small town near the
Dragoman Pass. It is late in November in the year 1885, and through
an open window with a little balcony on the left can be seen a
peak of the Balkans, wonderfully white and beautiful in the starlit
snow. The interior of the room is not like anything to be seen in the
east of Europe. It is half rich Bulgarian, half cheap Viennese. The
counterpane and hangings of the bed, the window curtains, the little
carpet, and all the ornamental textile fabrics in the room are oriental
and gorgeous: the paper on the walls is occidental and paltry. Above

the head of the bed, which stands against a little wall cutting off the right-hand corner of the room diagonally, is a painted wooden shrine, blue and gold, with an ivory image of Christ, and a light hanging before it in a pierced metal ball suspended by three chains. On the left, further forward, is an ottoman. The washstand, against the wall on the left, consists of an enameled iron basin with a pail beneath it in a painted metal frame, and a single towel on the rail at the side.[1]

And the description goes on and on to include props and set pieces that would drive any designer to distraction. These directions prescribe that the play be done in a realistic manner, and we will anticipate that the production as a whole will reflect the nuances and worldview that Shaw prescribes. In *Paper Wings* (1995), I offer the following:

The scenic requirements should represent various interior settings, but the composition of props and furniture should have a definite unreal quality in their placement to each other. A living room should be able to become a hotel room or a garage or whatever with a small change—keep things open and suggestive.[2]

This suggests the style of the play as being something more than Shaw's realism. In other words, you are not only providing a way into the "how to's" of pulling the production off, but also describing the more general stylistic intent of the play. Perhaps you have written a scene with a tank appearing on stage and you want to suggest the tank but also depict the characters inside the tank. Your stage description might go something like this: "A tank appears on stage which contains a tank crew. One character will hold up a facsimile of a tank cannon, but the others will be sitting on boxes mounted on a wheeled platform, which rolls onstage to the deafening sound of grinding tracks."

The stage set directions for *Everywoman* (2013) immediately alert the director to the variety of stylistic choices which are available in this multi-scene semi-futuristic drama.

The Set

A television station talk show host set.

When characters step off the television set proper they can go anyplace or anytime. Gracie's make up room is a chair, a wastepaper basket. Most locations are accomplished with a change of lights and sound. A red light will indicate when the talk show set is live.[3]

A playwright must be open and sensitive to all kinds of input: the visual is by no means secondary. If you understand the conventions, you will also help your reader/producer understand what the rules are that you play by, and why they are important. If you want to contribute to the feel of your play and how it is produced, you need to develop a singularly strong and workable overall set image for the producers to relate to.

## Play Formatting

Unlike writing for film, there are a variety of formatting choices that exist for the stage. Two examples are offered below. In looking at the following, note spacing, the use of margins in parentheticals, italics when used, when names are capitalized, and so forth.

## Example One: The Classic Approach for a Script Read in Professional Circumstances

### SCENE ONE

(JOHN enters, flustered, fumbles in his pocket for his wallet, and looks helplessly at BILLY behind the counter.)

JOHN

One hamburger . . . but I can't pay for it, all of it that is. Put cheese on top.

(sighing)

I just ran away from my rehearsal dinner.

(BILLY slaps a hamburger on the grill.)

BILLY

(clucking his tongue)

Ran away . . . whaddid I teach you? You always run towards somethin.' Never away.

(blowing his nose)

'cept in Springtime when the ragweed comes out. Then you run . . . your nose runs, your eyes run, and all you want to do is run to the

North Pole.

(JOHN pulls out a soiled hanky.)

JOHN

(apologetic)

Here. It's all I got.


## Example Two: This Emulates What Most Publishers Use

THE SET

*(The year is 1716, Penn's birthday in Ruscombe, a smallish country estate in England. The set is located in a barn, with farm implements about, hay, and at one end of the barn an elevated area which has been turned into a temporary stage platform on which Penn's children are going to enact scenes from his life. The children have erected a hanging curtain out of pieced muslin with an array of props to use in the 'drama.' The children have created a straw effigy, dressed in period clothes, a sort of glorified scarecrow.)*

SCENE ONE

*(The barn. THOMAS (16) is fencing a straw effigy with a rusty sword. MARGARET (14) is lighting some lanterns, getting props ready. Masks and costume pieces are hanging about.)*

THOMAS: Stand and deliver, knave. Your money or your life.

MARGARET: Stop it! Quakers don't wave . . . those things around. And we don't steal money.

THOMAS: (*to effigy*) Aye, then fork over your tobacco.

MARGARET: We don't . . .

THOMAS: Papa smokes a pipe. And he drinks brandy, and I've seen him with one of these in his study, doing this . . .

MARGARET: You haven't . . .

THOMAS: I have when he didn't know I was watching.

MARGARET: Just put it away, Thomas. If Papa catches you . . .

THOMAS: You mean, Maman . . . Is she coming?

MARGARET: Maybe later. I see Richard and Papa on their way here . . . now. Take this end . . .

> (She has a sign roughly painted with felicem natalem! that she is unraveling. He grumbles but helps.)

THOMAS: He won't remember, anyway.

MARGARET: Who cares . . . because . . . it's his . . . birthday.

> (And with that they unfurl the banner/sign with the Latin phrase.)

THOMAS: He won't like it. He'll look down his nose and say, 'where are the poor?—give a party for the poor and I'll come.'

MARGARET: Well, Maman said that we're poor. . . mostly. Shhhh.

> (PENN enters, blindfolded. He is dressed in a dressing gown over simple vest, pants, loose high collared shirt. Wig is slightly askew. He still has his nightcap on. RICHARD (10) is leading him. He breathes deeply.)

Unlike film formatting, theater has a host of different formatting choices, and all have made their way into the publishing arenas. Pick one that provides the most comfort and clarity and speed for you. It would benefit you to also research the publishing company that you are approaching and come as close to their formatting in submitting playscripts.

## Aristotle and Dramatic Action

The *Poetics* is essentially about the structure of Greek tragedy. It was Aristotle who started the play structure and composition ball rolling in the fourth century, and thus deserves the recognition as the first dramatic critic of western civilization.

With typical Greek rationalism, Aristotle approaches dramatic storytelling as a science. He begins with the idea of plot as the soul of tragedy, and even though he is discussing tragedy, primarily Sophocles' *Oedipus Rex* (429 BC), his principles apply to all playwriting efforts.

*Plot* is the arrangement of the incidents. Incidents must have unity, which means that there is a cohesiveness in which character, thought, diction, and action come together on a single action or spine which predominates throughout the entire drama. In *Oedipus Rex*, the primary dramatic action is for Oedipus to find the killer of his father. Unity also means the implied likelihood and necessity of each incident. The incidents must be both probable and essential to the story. A story does not copy nature but is an imitation of it. Unity comes about from a logical cause and effect relationship between incidents. It ultimately contributes to and helps form the essential symbiosis between form and content.

A plot that imitates a whole life will lack form. The focus should rather be on a few condensed, significant, and meaningful incidents. The plot must also have order and magnitude—in this way they form a beginning, middle, and end. Magnitude means that it tells the whole story, and that the story or plot elements are congruent with the nature of the work. Put another way, look for big deeds involving city states and countries when dealing with a play that features kings and the usurpation of power.

The beginning, according to Aristotle, portrays a protagonist who is living a good life, but who has a significant character flaw. At the end of the beginning, there is a reversal of fortune. This reversal is not simply a fall from fortune, but a fall brought on by the character's own flaw. Two Greek words that define this process are *hubris*, or pride, and *hamartia*, or tragic flaw. You could very easily begin with a character who is not necessarily good, who is a reprobate but who ultimately desires something worthy in terms of ethical veracity. This character's arc, or journey, then is going to be more challenging and interesting to watch. For tragedy, it works toward the opposite: a good man who through a flaw has a considerable fall.

The middle of the play takes place as the protagonist fights against his change in fortune, but at the end of the middle he recognizes his error. He changes from ignorance to knowledge, but it is too late.

The end presents a catastrophe that brings on great suffering and which results in catharsis or soul cleaning, if not for the protagonist at least for the audience. And a new order is established.[4]

Dramatic action is the key, with an understanding that drama is not just outward conflict, but conflict played out by characters in a progressive manner building to a climax that is meaningful and moving. As such, this concept of action deserves a bit more explanation. As we move to film, we are overwhelmed with the abundance of action thrillers characterized by Jack Ryan, James Bond, and superheroes galore. We are subjected to marvelous displays of relentless action, but often at the expense of character development and motivations which reflect individual consciousness and strategies that harbor flaws, fears, and self-destruct mechanisms. Change is brought about by external forces, seldom by internal struggles which bring to the surface unconscious goals and objectives.

And then there is the nature and make-up of those forces which contend with the wants and needs of the protagonist. This is your antagonist. It can be an act of nature, it can be one's own psychological vagaries, but it is best expressed with a face on it as an antagonist character that can be interacted with—no conflict, no obstacles equals no interest. And the more your main character must go through from the standpoint of inner and outer struggles related to his goal or objective, the more interesting the story. In *Oedipus Rex*, the antagonist tension comes from many sources: from his own backstory in which he murdered his father and married his mother, from a plague that is crippling the city of Thebes, from a seer who prophesizes his end, from the gods, and finally, from personal pride. It is a tragedy to be sure, and the tragic catharsis arrives as we identify with a noble man who survives and realizes his own guilt in which an array of conflict elements have brought him down.

The action of a good play always points forward. Author Robert McKee calls this progressive complication, in which there is a logical and seemingly necessary cause and effect movement whereby one scene leads organically to another, and which serve as vehicles for suspense, emotion, and the sense that all is accelerating toward some inevitable and meaningful conclusion.[5]

This is your climax, which is characterized by the most intense action as the protagonist faces the antagonist directly, and where your main character is tested to the maximum in realizing the objectives that were established in Act One of the drama. It is also where the theme or issues are brought into the clearest and sharpest focus and proved through action. The final reaction of an audience to a dramatic action, perfectly rounded out and complete, is not really one of surprise, however stunned they may be. Arthur Miller's phrase for it is "Oh God, of course!"

*The elements* which comprise this dramatic action movement are composed of plot points, character arc, dialogue, and more, and will be analyzed in subsequent chapters.

## Discussion Questions and Exercises

1. Conceive of ten different locations that you would like to set your play idea. It could be a bar, a church sanctuary, a bus stop, or a television studio. First, research pictures and artwork of these locations as done in paintings and found in real life. Write down what you find most interesting and useable from a story context.

2. Take the same ten locations and do a search to find how different stage designers have treated the same location. How does their treatment reflect the mood and reality of possible story elements?

3. Select a play that you enjoy and that might be congruent in some way with the play you are thinking about writing. For example, you might select *Desire Under the Elms* (1924) by Eugene O'Neill. Note how different designers have treated the same play in terms of design conceptualization. What do these differences connote? Other plays to consider might be: *Waiting for Godot* (1952), *A Midsummer Night's Dream* (c. 1596), and *Story Theater* (1970).

4. You have a story idea for a play. You see it in your head. Do a search and locate pictures of theatrical sets that you feel most aptly capture what you are going after. Perhaps your play is set mostly in a barn, or a television studio, or a haunted castle. How do these various representations feed your writer's imagination?

# Chapter 7

# The Premise Statement and
# Story Idea Development

THE *PREMISE STATEMENT* IS A BRIEF PARAGRAPH that captures the feeling, the flow, and the intent of your play idea. It does not consist of the entire plot, nor does it provide dialogue or complete character descriptions. Think of it as a vehicle; if someone asks what your play is about, this premise statement will answer their question, or at least lead to a further conversation. Some writing texts say that it should be one sentence, but I like to have it include more of your story to truly entice the reader or listener to want to hear more. If you can communicate a good story idea in three sentences or so, then it implies you have probably put together the beginnings of a good story.

Let me emphasize a few principles of writing a good premise statement, also called an extended log line.

- Since you often do not include what happens in the end, the body of the premise must really grab your imagination. Too often the body is predictable, and not really a story. So your audience has given up even without knowing the climax. You need to excite your readers' imagination in terms of wondering what will happen.

- Do not write a career pattern. Do not write about a state of being. Write about a gripping or moving or funny dramatic action through situations that promise more excitement than you can generate in two lines or so. Think of specific dramatic events rather than states of being.

- Do not be afraid of writing what will happen at the end. If it is a phenomenal ending and you have it down, find a way to share it with whoever you are communicating with.

- Be concise. Frame the action and conflict in your description. The audience needs to know the problem. If it is too parochial you will see them lose interest in a moment. Consider this example from *Oedipus Rex*: A proud young ruler sets out to find the killer of the

King of Thebes—but he discovers that he is that killer and that the King was his father, and he subsequently blinds himself.

There are three parts to a premise statement: first, there is the character, "A proud young ruler." Second, there is the action or premise "sets out to discover." Third, there is the consequence: "blinds himself." Another example comes from *One Flew Over the Cuckoo's Nest* (1975): A profligate but sane man is sent to a mental institution and learns the hard way— that the head nurse is a lot more dangerous than the patients. He is driven to leading his own personal insurrection—the result? Freedom for another inmate, and a lobotomy for his own self-sacrifice.

Another example: a young college student becomes fascinated with the story of the end of the Mayan calendar. Abandoning everything, he travels to Belize to study the ancient civilization, discovering terrible secrets of the end of the world. Can he warn others in time to save life as we know it? Here, there is a protagonist with a goal. The stakes are high. We can imagine the obstacles. Time is running out. There is a mystery. What more do you want?

An example of providing a bit more information is included below, outlining the play I wrote titled *Brendan's Journey* (1997):

Brendan, sixth-century monk, accompanied by his nemesis and half-brother Birt, sets sail in a pirogue to discover that great land over the sea. Haunted by his passion to spread the Gospel, and inwardly questioning how God could dwell within, Brendan confronts wild weather, volcanoes, Judas on an ice flow, madness, and doubt, as a sojourner on the ocean. He makes it there and back again, but only to discover a secret more moving and revelatory than all the adventures offered up by sailing the ocean.

## Developing the story for your Full-length Play Idea

Hopefully you have been inspired and, out of the fog of your creative imagination, characters are beginning to strut about, a theatrical set or sets are beginning to emerge, and you have something you want to say and some idea of the context within which you want to say it. You are now ready to set down your story idea. An outline of the various aspects is provided below, with accompanying explanations, and with a debt to Dr. Buzz McLaughlin.

### Story/Play Idea Outline

**Premise Statement**. (See above examples.)

**Play Title**: Titles are important. Put down two or three if you are not sure.

**Main Character**: (Name, age, occupation, and objective—what does your character consciously want? Hedda, from Henrik Ibsen's *Hedda Gabler* (1891), wants to totally control the men around her. Hamlet wants to expose the killer of his father. Brendan wants to evangelize the land across the sea. Peter Pan wants to never grow old.

**Antagonist and Obstacles**: Who or what is trying to keep your protagonist from getting what they want? Describe the antagonist's objective, in other words, why does this person want to obstruct the hero's journey? What is in it for them? Can you describe at least one strategy that they will use to try and accomplish this?

**Climactic Action**: Briefly describe the final climactic confrontation between the central character and antagonist(s). This is not a discussion between them. It is a complex of meaningful and life changing actions.

**Why Did You Pick This Story?** In other words, what are the meanings or theme values in your story that make you want to tell it? Why is it important to you today?

**Time and Place:** In what time period and location does this take place? The year 2030? After an electro-magnetic pulse (EMP) attack, in Dayton, Ohio?

**What Are the Primary Sets that You See Being Used?** Interior rooms in Uncle Vanya's House? Picnic on exterior grounds, ending in outside the weathered house?[1]

It is important to remember that you are not locked into how you see your play evolving at this time. Things always change, but that is what makes it exciting. This story world that you have created should be working on you by this time. You will think about it, scribble notes, puzzle over it, and laugh and cry. But that is what a good story is supposed to do.

It is also important to note that this prior emphasis on plot points and synopses and treatments is not a formula to be followed. In the passion of writing, you pour out the play on paper, but maybe it is not working quite the way it should. Now is the time you go back and look at plot points and beats and see if they are doing what they should be doing.

## Discussion Questions and Exercises

1. Apply a premise statement to your three favorite plays. Model them after the *Brendan's Journey* example provided in this chapter.

2. Write out the premise statement for a play you have written or that you plan on writing.

3. Address the categories listed in the development of your story/play idea outline.

4. Can you come up with character objectives? Can you see the climactic action happening at the various plot points?

# Chapter 8

# Creating Your Characters

ARISTOTLE HAS ALWAYS BEEN CONSIDERED A STRUCTURALIST. This could mean that he favors plot as a dominant element in storytelling, without which you would not have a coherent sequence of events, and, therefore, if a story emerged it would probably be suspect. This is something of a bad take on Aristotle, who does talk about form and content in terms of character development.

So, what comes first, plot or character?

One of those who advocates character as predominant is Lagos Egri in his book *The Art of Dramatic Writing: Its Basis in the Creative Interpretation of Human Motives*.[1] Others might say that they could not have conceived of a play or film without first having an overwhelming image that they experienced out of which plot and character would grow. Examples of pure plot driven pieces would be Roman comedy since farce has a built-in prevalence for intricate plot twists. Add to these the popular Hollywood action-adventure thriller as a film genre and you have models for the plot-dominated drama appearing throughout the ages.

In William Shakespeare's *Hamlet* (c. 1600), the Player King tells his wife:

I do believe you think what now you speak,
But what we do determines oft we break.
If we ourselves in passion do propose,
The passion ending, the purpose we do lose.
So, think thou will no second husband wed,
But die thy thoughts when thy first Lord is dead.[2]

Hamlet's entire struggle is with action, with deciding what to do. Ultimately, we measure the man on this basis: on his will to act; on the nature of the action; the cost of the action; and the success or failure of the action. Likewise, true character can only be determined insofar as we see it in the context of action, which challenges, tests, exercises, and ultimately judges moral choices.

Here you see the resolution to the argument: character and action become, essentially, indispensable to each other.

Just what is this element of writing called *character*? To simplify greatly, when character is mentioned, two aspects come to the forefront: (1) *characteristics* or *caricature* (surface indications of character), and (2) *deep character* (or character revealed or developed under the demands of action.)

*Characteristics*, or *caricature*, are what might be referred to as the surface of "what we see"— labels that can be attached to people as we first encounter them. These are people's idiosyncrasies, their surface level psychological attributes, their habits, and their rituals.

Because characteristics are surface level it would seem they are not important. But they are important because they remind us that even the saints are grounded in the very idiosyncratic. We are not perfect. We are differentiated. These characteristics often point toward a deeper character element than what at first glance appears on the surface, which might look like just a character type.

Such successful dramatists as the Greek and Roman comedy writers, William Shakespeare, Molière, the *commedia dell'arte* (a sixteenth century form of popular theater that emphasized ensemble and improvisational acting), and Ben Jonson, to name several, have created plays that feature characters of exceptional vitality and who display characteristics of a singular passion, whether it be lust, appetite, cunning, hypocrisy, bombast, or miserliness, and take it to the extreme. Physical knockabout, blatant sensory preoccupation, and the inability to escape their consuming flaw provide a kind of comic justice as they end up paying a price for their excessiveness. We laugh at them, and secretly hope that we are not prone to the same self-blindness exhibited in our own foibles and fancies.

*Character*, on the other hand, is what the character does under pressure. Therefore, we create plot points and obstacles for the character so that she can face the flaws within herself and hopefully still find the resources to move toward her goal. When Aristotle mentions dramatic action, he is talking about the hero confronting a variety of challenges that test both his inner and outer self, and which also have an ultimate meaning in terms of the values involved in the action pursued. This, of course, is what we seek to create and resolve through action.

## Three Approaches to Character

Three approaches to the idea of character viewpoint and action variables are noted below: (1) the egocentric, (2) the interactive, and (3) the environmental or contextual. These are influenced by Robert McKee's treatment of the levels of character interaction.[3]

## The Egocentric

The *egocentric* projects the inner life of the character: the thought life, ego, and subconscious at work. When you become familiar with the proclivities of how your character thinks at the most personal (and not always directly expressible) levels, then you are prepared to drop this character within the matrix of your burgeoning story. We judge what we think about the inner mind by the outer actions. But there are a few things we can note when we are thinking of what is going on inside.

- How does this character you are creating think? Logically, emotionally, or imagistically? Why does this character think this way? Is it from genetics? Does competitiveness run in the family? How about artistic proclivities? Could it also have been his environment: his rigid ways having been drilled into him by his strict mother? Does this person make quick leaps of the imagination? Does he strive for syllogistic thought?

- What are the fears of your character? How do they manifest themselves in outward behavior? Will your character be able to face these fears and change because of the story conflicts you put her through?

- What is your character hiding? How does your character hide these things? Why is your character hiding these things? How desperate is your character to get these secrets out? Or to keep them hidden?

- What does your character hate about himself? What does your character love about himself? How do we discover this by what your character does?

- Sin blinders: What does your character do and think when she thinks God is not looking?

- What are the glasses through which your character observes the world? Does he wear the glasses of optimism, pessimism, cynicism, hope, exuberance, hate, anger, challenge, despair, or love? How is this reflected through both characteristics and character goals in your creation?

- Can you describe a dream of your character that is recurring?

- Does the character's personal idiosyncrasies stem from his inner fears and preoccupations? For example, your businessman has a gym set up in his office. He dyes his hair. He buys one of those automatic nose clippers and carries it with him. He is deathly afraid of growing old.

Another way of expressing the character's consciousness, especially in the theater, is the *outer monologue*, which is presented out loud as an extended speech in your script. An example would be Jake telling a story to Mary Lou about being thrown from a horse for the third time and what that means to him now, and that is why he is the way he is. He is afraid of her somehow "throwing him off." How to write the monologue is covered in Chapter 14 on Dialogue.

The *soliloquy* can also be used to express the character's consciousness. In the soliloquy, the character talks to himself or to the audience about personal things. Shakespeare's "To be or not to be. . ." is a speech which plumbs the depth of Hamlet's existential quandary. This literary conceit is seldom used in contemporary dramatic literature.

There is also the *inner monologue*, which the actor uses to ensure that they are "in the moment." This is the character's take on what is happening and is made up by the actor to ensure that they are always aware and concentrating on the action onstage. This is essentially said to themselves and is not heard by the audience. An example would be:

*(DENNIS slowly opens the attic door.)*

"Damn door, squeaks, supposed to be a surprise. Hot up here. She's asleep at her desk again, fingers all covered in ink. Wish she'd spend as much time with me. Maybe if I turn the fan on. Touch her hair first, dare I? Can't wake her. Won't wake her. Dying to wake her."

It becomes the writer's job, then, to provide a character with enough complexity that the actor can work comfortably and profitably within the established boundaries created. In other words, you do not write the inner monologue, but you have gone over semblances of this internally yourself during the writing process.

All the above represent different ways of getting into the intensely personal nature of character creation, either by the actor or the writer. It is story that reflects what we as audiences are most desiring to identify with.

It provides a fabric of motivations and inner dealings that makes the character truthful, vulnerable, and knowable. But what is most important about being able to elucidate these inner personal drives and secret thoughts is that they need to ultimately drive the character toward doing something.

Representatives from the Moscow Art Theater were in a short residence at Tulane University when I was a graduate student there. When asked if they could distill the renowned Russian theater practitioner Konstantin Stanislavski's technique down to its most important principle, their unequivocal answer was "physical action," or always doing or wanting to do something at every moment on stage. It is your responsibility as the playwright to fill your characters with wanting to do, to act, to change things, to get something, and to live in a state of active desperation.

Remember: All thought must lead to **Action**.

Remember: All feeling, or desire must lead to **Action**.

Remember: All action must lead to more **Action**, as well as ongoing reaction.

One of the ways to determine the course and depth of the action is through creating and complicating the drive for what the character wants (conscious), and what the character needs (unconscious), which is often subliminal, and which can take the length of the play to discover. This leads to divisions deep within the character that will need to be confronted by the Act Three climax. For example, Hamlet's "want" is to verify and carry out justice upon the killer of his father; his "need," however, is to be a lover to his mother and to usurp his father. It is usually the buried need element that reflects the psychological drive of a character's wants and needs. With Hamlet, his acceptance of death at the end of the play leads to his maturation and allows him to go beyond the so-called Freudian preoccupations which are keeping him from actualizing judgment on his father's killer.

The egocentric is often difficult to project consistently on stage or film, unlike the novel for example. On stage we are looking for interrelationships and events which establish the context for the story's development. We want a character who has the substance of an intense inner life, but we do not want to live with that for too long. It can become indulgent and even embarrassing. Plays and films are composed of subtext and actions which mirror the inner life, but which do not dwell upon it because the character needs to embroil herself in the exigencies of an activated life going on around her. Plot is built on the consecutive revelation of actions as well as thoughts, which tell the story in a variety of meaningful ways. This leads to the interactive, the second category of meaningful interplay of action dynamics that compose story.

## The Interactive

The *interactive* is composed of the important actions between your character and family, close friends, lovers, workers, and your enemies or antagonists. It is at this level that most of the action of your story will take place. All the subplots will originate in this aspect of character viability.

The egocentric nature of your character needs someone to relate to; someone he can talk with. So who are some of the most functional characters to have your character relate to? The following is a list of attributes that your antagonist and secondary characters could possess to reflect the inner life of your character's goals.

- Someone who is in potential conflict with your character.
- Someone who represents a different worldview than your character.
- Someone who will challenge your character.
- Someone who wants something your character has, or someone who has something your character wants.
- Someone who can be a mentor to your character.
- Someone who knows what buttons to push on your character.
- Someone who wants to stop your character or get him going in a different direction.
- Someone who your character is emotionally involved with.
- Someone who has a secret that will change the direction of your character.
- Someone who is the opposite of your character.
- Someone who will drive your character crazy.
- Someone who has a different value system than your character.
- Someone who your character desires.
- Someone who your character wants to run from.

You want characters with different voices, different motivations, different pacing, different mind sets, and different idiosyncrasies. "You mean,

I must get into the mindset of more than one character?" Absolutely. If you are in a prison, is everyone just a thug? No. Ask yourself what the characters know about each other. What is their history? Too often, beginning writers have two people meet and immediately start talking about things, relationships, or events that they have shared together and already know about. Sure, people do this sometimes, but it too often manifests itself as awkward backstory or clumsy exposition in your writing.

Let's say you are writing about a married couple. They have known each other for ten years and lived intimately with each other. They have learned what to say and what not to say. They have learned a love language. They have learned what buttons to push. They have learned how to manipulate. You never start from scratch. Good story is often about what is not said, or what is said sub-textually, that is, it implies something rather than stating it right out. Often your wants are being worked out at an interactive level while your personal thought life is manifesting itself at the egocentric level. Both areas are essential for effective storytelling. The inner motivational complex of your character, which is formed by background, worldview, and idiosyncratic thinking, are most effective when woven within a tapestry of emotion and memory. The true "who" of your personality becomes established here. The interactive immediately takes your story into the conflict arenas as your primary character contests, pursues, runs from, and learns from other characters who are designed to give form to the plot elements. In *The Odd Couple* (1965), Felix the neat guy and Oscar the slob are two friends of opposite temperament, living together as surrogate husband and wife, and they drive themselves as crazy as they must have driven their missing wives. Stanley and Blanche in *A Streetcar Named Desire* (1947) are thrown together as opposites which necessitates conflict. Stanley is the beast, Blanche the quarry. Stanley is instinct, Blanche is refinement and manners. Stanley is streetwise, Blanche is educated.

But there is still one more level of interaction that contributes to your necessary story character development: the environmental or contextual.

## The Environmental or Contextual

The *environmental*, or *contextual*, is the structured world in which you place your characters and its effect on the story. Few of us exist in a vacuum with no contact with the outer workings of this world. We spend a good part of our lives getting educated so that we can support ourselves in the various environments that we contend with. We are politicians, professors, students, engineers, farmers, shop owners, dock workers, and ballet dancers—the list goes on. Your environmental involvement shapes the direction that your plot takes as much if not more than your egocentric or interactive progressions. By contextual it is implied that you are doing something. Rather than talking heads, the idea is to project a matrix of activity that speaks to us in its own language. A maid is sweeping. Mabel is walking three invisible dogs. God is working at a forge and creating the universe.

It thus benefits you to know with some intimacy and particularization the worlds in which you place your character, be it a university professor dynamic in *Educating Rita* (1983), or a pre-World War II German fascist construct found in *Good* (1982). David Storey's play *The Contractor* (1970) is about the business of putting up and taking down a large wedding tent. Tom Stoppard's *Rosencrantz and Guildenstern are Dead* (1966) is about two secondary characters from Renaissance Denmark being dropped into the middle of the play *Hamlet*. Arnold Wesker's *The Kitchen* (1957) takes place exclusively in the kitchen of a busy restaurant.

Some of the aspects of environment which should be noted are as follows:

- Create environments that have the potential for conflict. At the opening of *Hedda Gabler* (1891) we know that Hedda will never be contained in Tesman's house. We wonder if Sally will ever be able to escape the lure of the Kit Kat Club in *Cabaret* (1966). In *Days of Heaven* (1978), we note that it is the blast furnace and environs like a hell's mouth that shape the human conflict which drives one of the protagonists to run.

- Create environments that work against the natural abilities of your protagonist and environments that will test your protagonist. Gus and Ben are tested and challenged by the expressionistic hauntings in Harold Pinter's *The Dumbwaiter* (1957). In Henrik Ibsen's *Peer Gynt* (1876), Peer blithely takes on the world and returns home to find his life has amounted to nothing.

- Create environments that are organic, that have an anthropomorphic quality, that reflect the psychological and physical state of the character. For instance, in *Eh!* (1955), a single actor play by Henry Livings, a shiny brass boiler in the basement takes on a character all its own and becomes the antagonist. Sam Shepherd's *True West*

(1980) features a house inundated by toasters which totally challenge its bland middle-class landscape.

- Think of the environment as a character, as someone who wants the protagonist to fail or to win. In Anton Chekhov's *The Three Sisters* (1901), the metaphoric movement of the women is that of being pushed out of the house as they desperately desire to get to Moscow, but they can never escape the trap that is their home. In the stage version of Herman Melville's *Billy Budd* (1941), the ship groans and traps the young sailor as he is manipulated by his nemesis Captain Vere.

- Create a new environment for the protagonist to appear in and be challenged by. Dorothy finds new friends and a surrogate family by going through the trials of Oz. Gogo and Didi are never able to figure out exactly where they are in Samuel Beckett's *Waiting for Godot* (1952), a metaphysical landscape that defines their existential angst.

- Let the environment be a place where something must happen. In the film *The Shawshank Redemption* (1994), prison has got to be about finding freedom. The cloying innocence of Nora's house in Ibsen's *The Doll's House* (1879) is also a prison to be escaped from. Jean Genet's *The Maids* (1954) has two maids enacting the killing of their mistress in her bedroom.

- Let the environment be full of surprises. *Brazil's* (1985) surrealistic setting is designed to keep one off balance, to juggle realities and states of being. The domicile of the middle-class Smiths in Eugène Ionesco's *The Bald Soprano* (1950) is a place where anything can and does happen.

As indicated above, the inspired use of environment also creates the seedbed for meaningful imagery in your story, which oftentimes aids the storytelling aspect of the narrative.

## Individualize Your Characters

*Differentiation* is the key word here. Bringing different types of characters together guarantees variety, conflict, and the potential for different points of view and additional subplots. If your character giggles a lot, put her across from someone who is deadly serious. Caliban in Shakespeare's *The Tempest*

(c. 1611) is a half-man, half-fish creature who bellows and rebels, and is presented in contrast to the more reticent Prospero, the stately sorcerer. Don Quixote, in *Man from La Mancha* (1965), is the aristocratic dreamer who is placed next to the portly and practical sidekick Sancho Panza. *Hamlet*, the student and thinker, is seen in contrast to Laertes, the explosive and temperamental youth of the same age.

Empathy is another important aspect of character creation. How will the audience identify with the character, his plight, his concerns, his attitudes, and qualities that mirror their own proclivities as they sit watching the performance? Involved here is primarily the emotional expression of the character as measured by believable development and ultimate expression. In a melodrama the audience cheers the hero, hisses the villain, and swoons over the lovers. Similar feelings, though hopefully under more restraint, should be experienced within by the audience identifying with the emotional touchstones in a more serious and complex drama. In this state of willing suspension of disbelief, we must understand and believe the feelings of the characters, if not identify with them. We have merged our own lives with theirs because of the enchantment and problems presented in the story. We want the hero to succeed. We want justice. We want understanding. We want to feel the drama as well as appreciate what is being said. Sympathy is not essential, but believability is. Macbeth is not necessarily a likeable character, he falls just short of being a serial killer, but at the end of the drama we are moved by the total emptiness and loss he experiences in the face of his dashed ambitions.

Do not let your characters talk about how and what they feel, find an action where the audience can see them frustrated or angry or resigned. The maxim of "showing not telling" reemerges here as an essential ingredient to good storytelling. To sum up, the audience does not have to like the character, but they need to empathize with him.

The various plot point crisis of the play should produce a visible change in the protagonist's behavior. This can involve revealing something that has been present all the time but cloaked or in denial.

Character development is the product of all the working characterization elements outlined above. William Archer, nineteenth century producer and director, calls it "unveiling," meaning it was present all along but hidden from the audience, that is, the secret. The action of the play is wrought up with the unveiling of the character's needs and desires.[4]

In getting to know your character inside and out, consider how you might address the following: what are the fears of your character? How do they manifest themselves in outward behavior? Will your character face these fears and change because of the story you put her through? I think loneliness is perhaps our greatest fear as human beings. It is the fear of having no one, of being totally by ourselves. Christ tells us through Paul that it is essential that we belong to a body, preferably the body of believers (see 1 Cor. 12:12–27). This is, in part, an answer to this loneliness. But within this context there still can remain a depression and loneliness in our hearts though we are surrounded by Christ followers. Where does this come from? Perhaps it is God's echoing cry telling us that we need to know him better, deeper, and that he wants to be our constant friend and companion?

Paul writes in 2 Timothy 4:16 (NIV): "At my first defense, no one came to my support, but everyone deserted me. May it not be held against them." We are contained within ourselves. We can only guess at what other people are really thinking. So we write in order that we may share with the community of humankind our deepest thoughts. At the same time the actual job of writing is a lonely one. You are by yourself, with yourself, and nobody else is around. But very quickly your writing, when it gets in the hands of artists, actors, and directors, will be the basis on which a community, however fragile and ephemeral, will be formed. Even our Lord Jesus was tempted by loneliness. In the garden before his trial, he says "My soul is overwhelmed with sorrow to the point of death. Stay here and keep watch with me" (Matt. 26: 38, NIV). He was close to begging his disciples to stand by him at this time. And on the cross itself, from the words of Psalm 22 (NRSV): "My God why have you forsaken me?" At this time, he knew total isolation and separation from the Father. He experienced a loneliness that we cannot even imagine. So we write on, but we long for the oneness we will have with the living God in knowing Him in eternity.

## Character Arc

All these character possibilities point toward the idea of change in protagonists who, after the trials and tribulations they are subjected to, evolve into someone who is more aware of themselves, their fellow human beings, and their environment. They have learned something. It is too easy in this life to end up in a rut. We have experienced it in ourselves and in others. Often, a good story will feature someone who is denying or leaving this rut, which could be personal attributes, destructive relationships, or the routines of work in environments that they desperately need to get out of. All of this requires change, one of the elements under consideration in Chapter 4.

This process of change can be mapped out through the creation of a *character arc* for your protagonist. Remember, the idea of legitimate change is at the heart of character arc. Otherwise, there is not any change, just a shift in circumstances. The change we are looking for is in the character, because that is what gives us hope.

Is your character pursuing an objective which will lead them toward a higher sense of virtue? In other words, are they pursuing a goal which challenges who they are at the beginning of the story, and which takes them through a journey that reveals to them that they are more valuable, and that life in general is worth more than what they started with? This implies that your character has the potential for change, that they consciously or unconsciously desire something that is beyond their reach and which, in obtaining, will stretch them in terms of ethical behavior and understanding. Hopefully, they will be proactive characters. In other words, they are the kind of people who make things happen. If they begin as reactive and on the run or avoid their destiny (e.g., Marty McFly in the film *Back to the Future*, 1985, and Jonah in the Old Testament), then it is the job of the character arc to transform them into proactive characters who stop running and actively pursue their goal. It is common to have a reluctant hero in your story who confronts his flaw through an action moment of self-revelation that involves change through new motivated awareness. These are often your plot point moments and involve intense conflict. The character arc should also progressively complicate the three aspects of character expression that form the core of your character: egocentric, interactive, and environmental.

Sometimes this change results in negative values being brought to the surface rather than positive ones. Again, Jonah, the reluctant prophet in Scripture, is changed at the end of his Nineveh experience into being even more unfocused in his personal relationship with God. His inability to change and rejoice with the Ninevites is his curse (Jonah 4:8–11). Michael Corleone in the film *Godfather III* (1990) ends up having lost his personal sense of conscience. Each of these characters change, but rather than being praiseworthy, the changes end up portraying characters who are more destitute and lost in their disassociation from themselves and their surroundings. In the play *Hedda Gabler*, Hedda imagines herself as the head of a

100

male worship cult and ends up committing suicide as she becomes trapped in her own misguided indulgences.

## Emotional Change

Learning how to feel is a key element that indicates a process toward change. Christian author and apologist C. S. Lewis's love story in the film *Shadowlands* (1989) moves from retribution and anger to forgiveness and even shades of hope. Hard-bitten materialist *Mother Courage and Her Children* (1946), in the play by Bertolt Brecht, moves audiences to tears with her silent scream over the loss of her children. Moving from hope to despair is the path that Beckett lays out for his lost clowns in *Waiting for Godot*. Jesus weeps twice that we know of—once over personal loss (John 11:35), once over Kingdom loss (Luke 19:41–44).

## Cultural Change

At the other extreme of this is cultural change. For example, the poet who becomes a businessman in *The Reluctant Fundamentalist* (2007); the erudite professor who falls in love as she is dying of cancer with the male nurse in the play *Wit* (1995); the working class English student who ends up transcending her instructor in *Educating Rita*; the out of work steelworker who ends up building a cathedral in *Miracle Mile* (2008). These are all examples of characters triumphing in areas which are truly challenging and not anticipated.

## Ethical Change

If the character arc is doing what it is supposed to do, then your characters will often discover a deeper reason why they are pursuing the goal that they have been launched on. This involves moral or ethical change. Natural law is imprinted by God in our brain and hearts, directing both us and the dramatic characters toward a hoped for natural good. The worlds of film and theater often forbid looking at incest, or murder, or perhaps even adultery as positive forces. Where is your character as an ethical being at the beginning and where at the end? For example, Caesar, the hero ape in the film *War for the Planet of the Apes* (2017), begins his journey seeking revenge but ends up showing mercy on his antagonist and becoming the savior for his community. In *Peer Gynt* the mischievous character of Peer begins his journey in search of power and wealth and ends up realizing that his life has been like the search for the heart of an onion—you just keep tearing off the layers until there is nothing left. The discovery could also involve a revelation about oneself, about potential that has been dormant, and the resulting "ah ha" moment caps the character arc. Such is the moment when the troublemaker McMurphy in *One Flew Over the Cuckoo's Nest* (1975) sacrifices himself for a select number of inmates at a repressive mental asylum.

## Family Change

The family is a biological, procreative, and childrearing structure. In dramatic works, some families are destroyed while others flourish. A family traditionally shares goals, values, and long-term commitments. It represents the basic building block of dramatic writing. And it moves easily into representative forms: the family as a sports team; the extended family that can exist in trailer parks; surrogate families that come about when diverse characters are placed in highly conflictual situations. The pursuit of completing missing elements in the family structure is a common subconscious desire within a protagonist's or antagonist's goal or objectives. Watching Edward Albee's *Who's Afraid of Virginia Woolf* (1966) in which a two-person family tears itself apart and then, with what love remains, puts itself back together in a different way, is an example of this. In *Long Day's Journey into Night* (1941), the family is in the latter stages of dissolution, and we watch with trepidation discovering the secrets and misunderstandings that propel it to its final point of separation. In Scripture, Joseph faces his brothers in Egypt and forgives them in a moving scene of exposure and forgiveness (see Gen. 42–45). This family then becomes a nation.

## Physical Change

Finally, in terms of character arc, look for physical changes in your character. How do their dress, their new relationships, and their acquired changes in perspective manifest themselves both in their own physical presence as well as their physical environment? David transforms from shepherd to King. Prince Hal in *Henry the IV, Part 1* (c. 1597) does a similar transfer from reckless Prince to proper Prince. Lear, the king in *King Lear* (c. 1606), is stripped of every royal benefit by the end of the play where he has left the role of repentant father. Stanley, the prodigal musician, ends up leaving his escapist pajamas and being brutally dressed in formal clothes but also in a catatonic freeze at the end of Pinter's *The Birthday Party* (1958).

## Character Flaw and Fears

What is the character's flaw? What is keeping the character, within herself, from getting what she wants? How has she dealt with this flaw by the end of the piece? This decidedly human identification factor in your story can be at the heart of your protagonist's journey, and her ability to overcome it or to use it in some manner is a determining element. Hedda's flaw in *Hedda Gabler* is that she wants to control the lives of everyone around her. Her flaw gets the best of her, and she cannot face a life that makes her a victim rather than a perpetrator. In *Oedipus Rex* (429 BC), Oedipus's flaw is pride, and he is humbled but in the process finds his true humanity. Sally's flaw in *Cabaret* is that she cannot give up the adoration she receives in the Kit Kat Club, and in the end, she sacrifices her child, loses her love, and condemns herself to a life of performing for a corrupt German populace.

Oftentimes the measure of the character is in how he succeeds—or not—in overcoming his flaw or flaws in the Act Three climax. God's revelation of character flaw in Scripture is unique to depictions of character in other religious tomes. Abraham, Joseph, David, Gideon, Jonah, Jezebel and Ahab, Michal, Moses, Rahab, Peter, Thomas, and Paul, to name several, all suffer some traits that form character, motivate action, and are addressed in God's unfolding story in Scripture.

## Change of Consciousness

As a species we are blessed with various attributes that shine through us as being made in God's image. These are qualities that I believe are at the heart of effective change within individual or societal units, and are worthy goals to pursue in awakening God-consciousness in your characters and your audiences. Some of these could include:

- **Awakening self-consciousness** by having your characters pursue questions of identity: Who am I? Why am I here? What do I want? How can I change my circumstances for the greater good? These remain as questions that are at the heart of our ultimate purpose and meaning in life.

- **Enhancing your character's responsiveness** to beauty and the call of moral responsibility for her actions.

- **Envisioning your character's future** and developing the potential acts to change it.

- **Increasing the character's ability to love other persons** even to the point of self-sacrifice.

- **Developing your character's sense of cause and effect, of Destiny beyond himself,** a reality which one pursues with all his will; a reality which seeks the mysteries of existence and goes beyond his present temporal and spatial boundaries, and is built into the fabric of our human consciousness.

The world of character creation is filled with an endless variety of types, of contrasting personalities, of noble and less noble goals, of the revelation of human truths and of the ongoing search for representational and symbolic truth as worked out through human beings who are capable of love, sacrifice, and equally capable of self-centered destructiveness. This journey needs structure, which becomes the vehicle for presenting those areas of challenge and contention so that they increase in terms of being increasingly more complicated. The basic building block for this structure begins with the idea of the beat, which provides the rational and dramatic material for the most elemental conflicts in your drama. This will be discussed in greater detail in our next chapter.

## Discussion Questions and Exercises

1. Characteristics are the outward building blocks of your physical and psychological character. With reference to the text's discussion, note any characteristics of the characters in your play story idea. How do these physical attributes also reflect the inner life of the character?

2. In getting to know your character inside and out, address the following questions: What are the fears of your characters? What are their flaws? What are they hiding?

3. Write an inner monologue for your protagonist or antagonist. This works best if it takes place at a plot point transition moment. Take your inciting incident and write what your character is saying, and then in parentheses write what the character is thinking. The success of this exercise is knowing your character's inner reactions in detail.

4. We all are influenced daily by where we live, travel, or work. Apply the following environmental or contextual factors to the play idea you are creating.

   - Have you created environments that work against the natural abilities of your protagonist, and that will test your protagonist?

   - Have you created environments that are organic, that have an anthropomorphic quality, that reflect the psychological and physical state of the character?

   - Is the environment a place where something must happen?

5. Character arcs chart the character's journey in terms of change, otherwise there is not any change, just a shift in circumstances. The change we are looking for is in the character, because that is what gives us hope. Subject at least one of the characters you are creating to the arc categories of change provided in this chapter.

# Chapter 9

# Play Structure and the Beat

WITHIN THE WORLD OF STORY CREATION there is some ambiguity in terms of just what a *dramatic beat* is composed of and how it works. Certain structural experts typify it as being a list of the overall progression of plot points ending with your Act Three climax—each plot point being a beat. In some dramatic texts, beat is referred to as a generic pause, nothing more. In this chapter, I define it as being the common denominator building block for the writer, the director, and the actor in the creation of a dramatic text and a theatrical production.

The idea of a beat, or the smallest motivational unit, is at the basis for all creation and can serve as a paradigm for the creation of much of art also. From a basic creational model, the beat can be seen as analogous to the molecule—not the atom. Why? Because the molecule is a more complex identifiable form which is attached to other molecules, and which can change radically as they interconnect. The basic nature of the atom never changes unless under the stress of nuclear fusion. But dramatic beats offer a variety of permutations and combinations and are constantly changing in terms of emphasis, meaning, rhythm, and pacing.

Konstantin Stanislavski, Russian theater practitioner who pioneered a system for actor training, preparation, and rehearsal, is the first person who is attributed with the use of the word "beat." When Lee Strasberg and Cheryl Crawford (Actors Studio, 1930s) were in Moscow studying his methods, they misconstrued what Stanislavski was saying. He meant bits rather than beats.

## Why Do I Need to Understand Beats?

If there is an area of a performance which is vague, repetitive, unfocused, and confusing, then I contend it is probably because the beat work is not in the script, or has not been identified by the director and the actor and finally realized by the actor in performance. This becomes somewhat evident in auditions and in all written drama including classical texts.

In theater, the *beat* has been described as the time between when a character starts to pursue a goal and the point at which he achieves it, changes it, or stops pursuing it. It would also include a major strategy change in accomplishing the objective. This means that:

- The beat can be described in terms of the "I want. . ." of the actor and thus becomes a viable action which is accomplished or not accomplished. Thus, the beat is a unit of action.

- As a unit of action, a beat should be described with some sort of physical action terminology—i.e., verb—in mind. If the actor/character is going to pursue an action, then it should be defined at the beat level. "Joan's objective is to get the letter from Elliot, no matter what." She tries asking for it (BEAT). She tries being seductive with Elliot. (BEAT). She tries drawing a gun (BEAT). She breaks down and cries (BEAT).

- "The beats are more or less building blocks upon which the whole structure of the play rests."[1]

- Building blocks suggest that beats are putting something together, that their use is varied and should be involved with the building complexity of the drama. As building blocks, some are larger than others; some more decorative; some more supportive or foundational. So beats should have a natural in-built diversity, one next to the other.

- Overall, within a *French scene* you might have several beats. A French scene is defined as a scene that is determined in terms of main characters entering or exiting, of phone calls, and other dramatic happenings that radically affect the action of the story. Each beat would have an objective defined for each actor, which is what they want. This is always congruent with their *super objective*, which, in the overall arc of the play, is their dominant want. Within each scene there can be several beats. The beats are how the objectives are realized. They are units of action that the actor plays and should be identified by action verbs. The super objective in a play might be that Jim wants to control and dominate his entire world. In Act One he is trying to seduce the boss's daughter to marry her and to get power. The objective of the unit is "to seduce Gwendolyn." He first attempts to loosen her up by making her laugh. That is the first beat. This fails. He then tries to impress her by smooth-talking her. This shows some promise. This is the second beat. He then tries a touch on the knee. Physical seduction. This fails. This is the third beat. And so on.

• It is often effective to couch the beats in terms of physical actions that you perform to get what you want. Actors respond to immediate physically oriented action motivations. As a writer you need to write these action moments.

There are two types of beats. First, there are beats that work directly to build an action, and second, there are emotional beats that are more mood intensive, oftentimes revealing inner aspects of character in a more contemplative sense. For example, when Gertrude describes the death of Ophelia in *Hamlet* (c. 1600), her speech is a single mood beat; or Willy Loman's entrance at the top of *Death of a Salesman* (1949) when he first comes on stage, late at night, confused, distracted, and broken. The number of beats in this opening sequence reflect the state of mind of poor Willie.

It should be noted that in mood beats, you never ask an actor to try and play a mood. This is not an action motivation. Actor's play actions, they are always doing. So when Gertrude comes on, she might be in shock, she might still be overwhelmed by the images that she saw. She might be wet and out of breath from fishing Ophelia out of the water, but what is she doing? She could be doing several things. For instance, her speech is a cry for help to Claudius because she realizes that she also had thoughts of suicide herself. Also, she wants to get herself cleaned up, purged of the dirt from outside and the dirt from within. And she wants to make Claudius see the wreckage he has wrought. And so forth. You do not play moods, you play actions.

## Beats for the Playwright

The reason you write in beats is that you want your play to be made up of motivational units rather than isolated lines. It is also easy for actors to play beats. They understand them instinctively. If you do not write in beats, then what might your script sound or look like? It will seem very much like stream of consciousness. It will lack variety in purpose, variety in strategies for your characters, variety in tone, variety in mood, and variety in pacing. In other words, it will put your audience to sleep.

Sometimes a piece of stage business can be an entire beat. The character sees a note on the table, he approaches the table, decides to open the letter, reads it, crumples it up, and throws it in the fire (A BEAT). A beat might also be a page or two long. A woman wants her husband to wrap a present for their child. Her pursuit of that goal is a beat. Her reasons compose the element of the beat. She is running late, she has to change her clothes, and the child will be home at any moment. When she grabs the box, tosses it on the couch, and decides to wrap it herself, that is the end of the beat. If she breaks down and cries, would that be a strong enough change in strategy to motivate another beat? Probably not, especially if you play at the top of the scene that the possibility of crying and losing it is part of her personal tension at this point. But if her husband suddenly brings out a loaded pistol and tells her that if she says one more word, he is going to blow her head off, then that would probably motivate another beat.

You do not write necessarily thinking about beats, but when you are re-writing, and something seems wrong with your scene, look to the beat work. You are bored by what you have written. Nothing seems to be happening. You have not complicated the lives of the characters. At this point, go back and do beat delineations to try and determine what is wrong. Then you can ask the technical questions about the length, intent or purpose, and nature of the beats that you have written.

## Cutting Beats

Cut any beats in which the character repeats the same tactics in pursuit of a goal. For example, a character wants his sister to leave the room. His first tactic is to lure her out, his second is to threaten her, and his third is to insult her. If he threatens her twice, it is less effective than if he threatens her once. Cut that approach.

If you have characters or a play that does not seem to be going anyplace, then it is because you have not realized goal-oriented physical action beats for your characters. This leads to an understanding of the word *motive*. In drama, a human being is dynamic, a restless seeker of some particular end. The forces at work within her—her motives—drive her forward to do or to attempt to do something in the outer world: to achieve freedom, control nature, or create order and stability from chaos or change. If we are to understand a character in a play, then we must think of her not as a static collection of qualities—a still portrait—but as a doer. Are you writing characters who are objective or goal oriented? It is the beats that supply precise information about the goals and desires of the characters.

Putting too many beats in a scene, or too few, will directly affect the pacing and forward movement of your scene. Too many beat transitions can speed up a scene inordinately, and you might discover that the quick changing of beats implies that you have not provided enough motivational material to provide for effective beat builds. The result is that your production could have a choppy feel to it, like an engine turning over but not really engaging. Too few beats could mean that your scene is saying the same thing over and over, that the characters never seem to be moving on, and you run the risk of having a scene that is discussion rather than dramatically motivated.

One of the problems with identifying and working with beats is that if you have two characters on stage, each probably has different wants and different actions to accomplish their objectives. In the opening of *Death of a Salesman* for example, Willy wants to find out what went wrong out there on the road. At the same time, Linda is trying to comfort Willy, to calm him down, and to find out what happened out there. Their beat transitions will not necessarily be at the same place. So you are charting two different routes for your characters, but they are always intersecting. And one of them will be dominant over the other. Willy is more desperate than Linda, even though both characters have their own real and immediate concerns. The primary beats are those which are determined by the dominant character, and the motivation for most of your movement will be instigated around the needs and wants of your dominant character.

## The Beat Transition

Remember that a beat transition is almost always characterized by movement in terms of meaningful action. So write your beats with that in mind.

As the playwright, in terms of how you write beat transitions, are you consciously moving your characters around, having them pick up props or move in the scene? Are you bringing characters in or having them exit? Are you writing action in every beat transition? An important thing to remember about beat transitions is that they always involve a choice or choices by the character to be realized or explored. They always involve a change in direction, rhythm, strategy, or need. They almost always raise the stakes in the relation between the dominant and subordinate characters.

**Beats Example**: (the // is the marking to indicate where there is a beat transition.)

//       *(BILLYBOY comes out of the closet, with pieces of female clothing over shoulders, head, etc., startling MICAH.)*

      *[Note: Almost any time you have an entrance, a phone call, or an exit by a character that is in the action you have a new beat. MICAH'S literal action is to get BILLYBOY out of the apartment. His essential action is to establish dominance over BILLYBOY and to not let him know that he's scared]*

MICAH: What the. . .? You been there all along?

BILLYBOY: Smelling the moth balls.

MICAH: Whaddya hear?

BILLYBOY: I heard the pop of a champagne cork. I heard the rustle of crinoline.

MICAH: It's just you and me now, buddy. Time's runnin' out. We got to get movin'.

BILLYBOY: I heard hot breath over the prairie.

MICAH: Yeah, well, I always said you had an overactive imagination. That's one of hers, on your head, take it off. The briefcase is on the sofa . . .

BILLYBOY: And lipstick is on the glass, see?

MICAH: O.K. There was a lady up here. Nobody you know and none of your business. It wasn't her. See. She gave me the key. . . to use, with this. . . with this other dame. How in hell's name did you get in?

BILLYBOY: *(flashing his fingers)* Magic fingers. You taught me well. Grease job.

MICAH: You let me know what you're doing from now on, you understand? I don't like surprises. I'll get the case, and . . . we are on our way.

      *(MICAH starts for the door, begins to open it. BILLYBOY draws a pistol from an inner pocket, throws the glass so it smashes into the door.)*

//

      *[Note: NEW BEAT. Characterized by physical action and*

*a change in who is driving the action as Billyboy takes over
controlling the primary action beat. Micah was not successful
in establishing or ending his beat. Billyboy's literal action is
to keep Micah from leaving. His essential action is to make
Micah know that he (Billyboy) is in control now and that he's
dangerous.]*

BILLYBOY: Shut the door. Turn around, slowly. Sit down. You're not
going anyplace.

## Discussion Questions and Exercises

1. Identify writing beats: using the text of one of your favorite plays,
   break down 6-8 pages of the script into playwriting beats. Note
   the following: (a) How do the beats function as a mini-play with
   beginning, middle, and ending action indicators? (b) Are the beat
   transitions you identified characterized by physical action choices?
   (c) How do the beats complicate the forward movement of the plot?

2. Write the beat transition: break down a scene you have written or
   write a new scene that has at least three identifiable beat transitions
   in it. At the beat transition moments, have you applied the necessary
   action dictums described in this chapter in terms of creating conflict
   that moves your plot forward? Describe these moments in terms of
   action and change.

3. Beats and props serve as meaningful communication devices that
   help define the objectives of the characters in plays. Using the beats
   discovered in either number one or number two above, analyze
   the use of props within the beats, noting how they function during
   the beat transitions. In addition, try adding a prop or two passed
   between characters into your beat transitions and see how this helps
   to shape the action and meaning of your scene.

# Chapter 10

# Plot Points and Complication

BEFORE LAUNCHING INTO THE PARTICULARS of the creation of a synopsis and a treatment, it is necessary to understand how the various aspects of story structure function in terms of play development. How the various pieces fit together and the essential contributing attributes that each one of these pieces bring to the overriding story narrative that you are creating is of paramount importance to your work.

## Exposition

The opening pages of your script are where you introduce, through *exposition*, the backdrop to the world of your story. It is not necessarily where you introduce all your characters or even the primary problem of your drama. It is usually used as a way of foreshadowing what the main action might be, and locates the audience into the time, place, and beginnings of action that you will be developing. The challenge is to mask the information that you provide in such a way that the audience has to guess and hopefully anticipate what is suggested in your writing. An example of exposition that does not do this and is therefore truly flawed can be seen in Tom Stoppard's *The Real Inspector Hound* (1968), in which he is purposefully mocking play building itself through bad exposition. Mrs. Drudge answers the phone at curtain and says: "Hello, the drawing room of Lady Huldoon's country residence one morning in early spring." She notices another character, Simon Gascoyne, and starts talking to him:

> MRS. DRUDGE: Judging by the time, you did well to get here before high water cut us off for all practical purposes from the outside world.

> SIMON: I took the short cut over the cliffs and followed one of the old smuggler's paths through the treacherous swamps that surround this strangely inaccessible house.

> MRS. DRUDGE: Yes, many visitors have remarked on the

topographical quirk in the local strata whereby there are no roads leading from the Manor, though there are ways of getting to it, weather allowing.[1]

What makes this exposition culpable? First, it provides information as information not related to character or action. It also provides unnecessary information with the result that the sense of the character dialogue is forced and artificial. What is desirous in good exposition is the following:

- The information must be story oriented. Some digression is fine because it contributes to establishing the mood and feel of the story and the characters. But it should relate to the evolving story in some fashion or other.

- It should be communicated in such a way that the audience takes in the information not realizing it as such. "Send Rocky to break his fingers. Tell him I know he keeps the watches, it's O.K. Unless it's a Rolex. I get the Rolex."

- Let the audience know what is necessary through the process of foreshadowing future conflicts and issues.

- Expository devices should be invisible and can be embedded in context, or organic activity. For instance, imagine two characters are lifting weights. The expository device must be interesting in itself and supply an organic context as a vehicle for good exposition. "Eighty pounds is good. You're making a comeback, I see. Getting some pecks on you. It's about time. Never get to a hundred, like me, but progress is being made. Here let's put on another ten." One character is dominating with the implication that the weaker one has been ill or something.

- Conflict is a very effective device to use in imparting information to an audience. Characters accusing, denying, attacking, or defending, used in a discretionary manner, can be used as vehicles to carry a lot of information.

- Characters are often involved in actions in which they know what is going on. And even though we as the audience do not know exactly what they are talking about, we sense the importance and are keen to pick up clues. We sense that we are getting prepared for something of importance down the road.

- Any emotional element, if authentic, will allow characters to say things that they normally would not say. "I'm not crying. It's the pollen. The countryside. This house in the countryside. Close the windows. I can't breathe, George." Of course, she hates the house and George is suffocating her.

- An action with no dialogue. "Hedda Gabler walks through the room like a tiger, pacing. It's after midnight. Shadows. She takes out a cigarette and smokes it, shifting uncomfortably in a stuffed chair." This action illustrates the discontent of the main character in pacing, sighing, and her rebellious nature in lighting a cigarette. Her discomfort comes from the fact that she is pregnant and does not want a baby.

- A narrator is something of a cheap expository device, and should always be enveloped in a character who has a vested interest in having to tell the story and who plays a part in it.

What is important is that the action is moving forward, questions are being asked, and hints are being provided. The characters can fool us, making us think one thing while masking their deeper desires. They can lie, deny, and forestall, all of which encourage us to read between the lines.

Another important usage of good exposition is that it provides the atmosphere of your story idea and establishes the genre—e.g., comedy, serio-drama, farce, tragedy, melodrama, musical. What is the mood that you want to convey? In *Macbeth* (1606), Macbeth is at war and encountering the witches results in an ominous atmosphere charged with dire circumstances. In *Death of a Salesman* (1949), Willie Loman comes in after a road accident late at night, weighed down with his sales cases, and tries to explain to his wife what happened, and how his world is beginning to fall apart.

Start your play in the middle of an action, for this will help to establish both the context and potential conflict from curtain up. People are in the middle of moving in or out. A wedding is just over. A honeymoon is concluded. Someone is packing. Someone is leaving. It is late and a couple are just arriving home from a contentious party. Someone is getting ready to commit suicide. Someone is trying on their old wedding dress.

## Balance or Imbalance?

It is best to start your drama in a place of imbalance, which means there is not a status quo but levels of discontent, of people in the wrong place, of secrets being hidden, and of relationships in general being questionable. Problems are hinted at; things are not going quite right. Or, if things are too perfect, we suspect that this house of cards is going to have to come tumbling down. Often exposition begins to foreshadow the problems that characters are in, before the first plot points begin to take shape. This allows us to see the parameters of the play's initial psychological and environmental conditions so that we can compare them with how the story ends. Where do the characters start and where do they end up?

Every play is a journey, so we want to understand where we have been to better understand where we end up and how we got there. One example of story imbalance from Scripture is Joseph, who is the youngest brother and has inspired jealousy in his older brothers for being his father's favorite. Another example is Rahab, who has had run-ins with the local authorities and runs a questionable establishment. Something is rotten; there's been a killing of a king. Or what about the example of Pentheus in Euripides's *The Bacchae* (405 BC). Is Pentheus old enough to be a ruler?

## Plot Points

Story structure is based on the logical and meaningful construction of beats, which lead to scenes, which lead to sequences and Acts. The milestone events, reversals, changes, conflicts, and resolutions that shape your story are called *plot points*. They represent those essential places in your story in which your central character's goal or objective is challenged and confronted with obstacles that have to be overcome or the story does not move forward. These obstacles challenge the characters' egocentric, interactive, and environmental encounters in a progressively more complicated manner, and ultimately provide the elements which will test the central character's worth, wiles, and will. Determining the events or decisions that escalate a story's problem should be "job one" for the working dramatist.

You have come up with a great story idea. You have a premise that you cannot get out of your mind with characters that surprise you, challenge you, and ultimately that you fall in love with in one way or another. Your story has conflict, character arc, and a climax that you feel is worth bringing to an audience to enjoy as much as you have enjoyed creating it. It is unique, original, and tells your story. Now this story needs to be structured into an exciting series of escalating, logically connected, and climaxed events. This is essentially your plot structure—your order of events, the framework, the architectural plans for how your story will be revealed. This is the form of your drama and in it, your characters and the evolution of its conflict can carry the content or meaning of your story. It is ideas wedded organically to structure—that is where the impact of your story resides. Ideas without form are intellectual propaganda. Form without ideas is playing with blocks that might balance one atop the other, but which have no ultimate meaning, and you get tired of the game rather easily.

## Inciting Incident and Act One Climax

The *inciting incident*, or *point of attack*, is the scene where the action that defines the premise first coalesces. It is the beginning of the point of no return for your protagonist, in which he is confronted with a problem and must take action. Oftentimes that action can be found in the Act One climax. I prefer the term point of attack because plays will often have several inciting incidents, but only one of these can be termed the point of attack. It is a meaningful moment in time, so it reflects your general overall theme. It foreshadows and makes the Act Three climax of your play inevitable. In other words, the problem that the point of attack poses must be answered in some manner by the climax. The objective that the main character has at the point of attack must be satisfied in some way by the Act Three climax. The point of attack for *Oedipus Rex* (429 BC), for example, is when he decides to take up the challenge of finding the killer of Laius. The climax of the play is the self-revelation that he is the killer. The point of attack also serves as a possible *crisis moment* for your Act One climax. A crisis moment is an action that motivates the central character in a meaningful way toward an inevitable action. A good way to think of it is as the happening, event, or realization which usually involves a decision that launches your main character on his journey. It is also of enough weight to begin to line up the forces of antagonism against the completion of his journey being realized.

The point of attack is that bit of action which jolts your protagonist out of his regular routine. Usually, life is not going that well anyway, but this event really kicks it off. For instance, Hedda in *Hedda Gabler* (1891) finds out that Løvborg, a former lover, is in town. Being bored with her husband, she is activated now in a new direction. She is going after Løvborg. Hamlet (c. 1600) is told by the Ghost that his uncle killed his father. He spends an entire play figuring out what to do, but he is bent on revenge at that point in time. In the New Testament, it would be when Jesus is baptized and starts his ministry (Matt. 3:13–17). Several additional point of attack moments are listed below:

- *Peer Gynt* (1876), when Peer decides to leave town to fulfill his destiny and conquer the known world.

- *Who's Afraid of Virginia Woolf* (1966), when George warns Martha not to play the game after she informs him that guests are coming over.

- *Twelfth Night* (c. 1602), when Viola has been rescued from the shipwreck and begins the search for her brother.

- *Old Times* (1971), when Anna makes her mysterious entrance into Deeley and Kate's home.

- *A Streetcar Named Desire* (1947), when Blanch comes to New Orleans to stay with her sister, Stella, and her nemesis, Stanley.

- *The Caucasian Chalk Circle* (1948), when Grusha rescues the infant Prince during the revolution.

- *A Funny Thing Happened on the Way to the Forum* (1962), when Pseudolus begins his matchmaking efforts to obtain his freedom.

- *'night Mother* (1982), when Jesse initiates her plan to commit suicide.

Look for the point of attack to begin within the first twenty minutes (twenty pages) of your drama because it and your Act One climax should be completed by about 25% of your story. Why is this? If thirty minutes go by and your audience still has no idea why they are watching this play, what all the back story is about, or what the stakes are, they are going to languish and lose interest. The point of attack should always happen in the evolving action of the drama, not as a flashback, not before the story begins, and not offstage. For example, a woman was saved when she was eighteen. The play begins when the Devil challenges her at age thirty. Though the salvation moment was certainly a life changing one, it is the meeting with the Devil that kicks things off and offers her the variety of choices and decisions she needs to make for this story.

## Act Two: Progressive Complication and Mid-point Crisis

Too many first plays fail through lack of complication. They proceed in a relentless direct line to the outcome. Complications enrich a play, throw it into relief, make it more vivid, and prevent it from being palely one-dimensional in content. The familiar criticism of a play that it is "too thin" stems from the lack of complications.

The Second Act is the test of writers. It is what writers are for. It is the biggest problem area and uses the skills of a good writer most efficiently. In your play, your Second Act begins after your first Act climax. It continues through your mid-point crisis, which is often your intermission, and ends at your Act Two climax, close to the ending of your play.

You know your protagonist. You know his goal. What could possibly happen to your hero? Anything and everything. As fast as you can, think of possibilities, and jot down every wild idea. The beauty of brainstorming is that a bad idea can lead to a good idea, so do not break the creative chain by judging an idea too soon. Challenge yourself to be downright silly.

Writing experts believe in a mid-point around page sixty. This basically means that a new, major obstacle or real change in the story—perhaps a reversal—that ups the ante for the hero and raises her degree of difficulty about solving her problem is introduced.

Act Two is also fertile soil for developing subplots, which exist to support and enhance and complicate the lives of your central characters. Strategies are becoming more desperate, more varied, and hopefully your central character is moving ahead as he overcomes the antagonist's forces.

Complication in drama creates new circumstances. Hamlet inadvertently kills Polonius, his girlfriend's father, which motivates Ophelia's suicide and Laertes's return to kill him. New characters can appear: that former lover with her/your child in tow. Moreover, a certain aspect of one's character may begin to dominate, such as Macbeth's ambition. Your character is surviving in the wilderness and learning. Romantic comedies often create moments of mistaken actions and identities and introduce former lovers and ulterior motives not known before, which challenge the emerging romance between the heroes.

To create, maintain, suspend, heighten, and resolve a state of tension is the main object of the dramatist's craft. George Pierce Baker defines what this tension is all about:

Suspense means a straining forward of interest, a compelling desire to know what will happen next. Whether a hearer is totally at a loss to know what will happen, but eager to ascertain; partly guesses what will take place, but deeply desires to make sure; or almost holds back so greatly does he dread an anticipated situation, he is in a state of suspense, for be it willingly or unwillingly on his part, on sweeps his interest.[2]

Suspense often implies a developing reversal of fortune. In Henrik Ibsen's *The Wild Duck* (1884), when Gregers Werle enters Hjalmar Ekdal's house as a lodger, we know that he will challenge the secrets of everyone in it. Yet he does virtually nothing for a whole act. Ibsen knows that the audience will be leaning forward in suspense before Gregers makes his first move. Gregers Werle is the interloper, the human being looking for exposure of secrets and revenge. We know he is going to cause great trouble in Ekdal's household, but Ibsen draws out the suspense by having him not really pursue aggressively his action until later in the play. When I was writing a musical version of *Puff the Magic Dragon* for Paul Stookey, he wisely advised me not to bring Puff on too early in the drama, but to just hint at his coming and create suspense for the children in the audience.

Follow through on the questions of how, why, when, and where, and you will be planting questions in the audience's mind, and if the questions matter then you are creating suspense. All this stems from the original question(s) posed in Act One. For example, Joseph finds a money filled suitcase stashed in the trunk of his jalopy and decides to run and enjoy the benefits of his discovery. Will he get away with this and will his luck change? By the end of Act Two he has been found by the mob that planted it, made to join their forces, fallen in love with the gang leader's girlfriend, and is the fall guy for the next big heist.

It is also important to provide the audience with moments or interludes that provide breaks from relentless and challenging action. The movement patterns of a roller coaster provide a helpful analogy: the slow, squeaking rise up the hill, the fast descent, curves, and all of a sudden you are upside down. This is what comic relief provides and the development of subplots with secondary characters who have problems of their own. But different demands are being made on them, and this helps to provide the variety that is needed. You are never to lose this tension because it is the "through line" holding up the evolution of your action trail. We never stop asking ourselves about Joe Keller's "But I'm in business" line in Arthur Miller's *All My Sons* (1946) as his posited justification for being exonerated from culpable choices. In the brilliant film *Witness* (1985), the corrupt police are always there in the background ready to intrude on John Book's escape to the Amish countryside.

If we can predict the ending of a story early on, usually the author has not provided enough of the ups and downs and curves and obstacles to warrant our continuing on the adventure. If the protagonist keeps encountering the same problems and they are dealt with in similar manners, then you are usually stuck in Kansas when you ought to be somewhere in the Rockies.

The audience can know something terrible is going to happen, just not what exactly is going to happen. The simple fact of waiting creates tension. In *Waiting for Godot* (1952), Samuel Beckett sustains this tension throughout the whole play, because of course Godot never comes. Nothing may happen in the conventional sense, or no goal is reached, but high tensions are established, and internal conflict is kindled in the minds of the audience. And this is dramatic. A former Professor of mine, Richard Schechner, would liken this to electric shocks being exchanged between two oppositely charged poles, rather than a slowly building action resulting in an Act Three climax that provides insight and resolution. Much of "Theater of the Absurd" breaks the matrix of cause and effect in telling a story, but the shock effect helps to support the existential message formalistically. In this case prior action, psychological motivations, and change that is logical and easily identifiable no longer play a significant part in the story. But because they are absent, the meaning of the author's worldview is mirrored in the chaos of breaking the rules of more classical story structure.

The use of subtext in dialogue is another tool that the playwright uses in establishing tension. For instance, Mike is trying to seduce Melanie. They are having dinner. The way he eats his salad, or cuts his meat, provides a physical subtext to the scene in that he is trying to entice his date. He might talk about why he loves asparagus, bringing up the sensory aspects of preparing and devouring it. This provides an underlying verbal subtext that we—hopefully— subtly recognize and wonder where and how this is going to outwardly contribute to his objective.

All these suspense and tension factors are causing the central character to develop more revealing and desperate strategies to overcome the obstacles which the story organically offers up. They are indicative of the progressive complication that needs to constantly be moving the second act forward. Perhaps one of the most important moments in the story's action is the mid-point crisis which happens just before the play's intermission.

The questions we ask ourselves as we head out to the lobby during intermission are: how is he going to get the girl? How will he find out he is being set up? Will he go to the FBI and become a double agent to the mob? And what is this doing to the sensibilities of this poor college student who was just on the run from the law? What is being set up is the mid-point crisis.

The mid-point crisis usually comes just before the intermission since most plays today have one intermission, and the writer wants the audience to come back after the break being desperate to find out what happens in the rest of Act Two. If the play does not have an intermission, then the dramatic event of the mid-point crisis should still exist because it serves as a major change or reversal plot point in your drama. Since a play is often composed of fewer events than a film, having these crisis moments of revelation, mystery, reversal, and introducing new elements becomes very important. They help to ensure that your drama is always on its way to developing progressive complication. For example, a student of mine has written a play where a woman points a gun at a policeman chained in her basement who she has essentially kidnapped. Blackout. Gun shot. Did she shoot him? What is going to happen next?

Oftentimes the mid-point crisis, in the spirit of just about all plot points, is characterized by physical action. The characters are doing something rather than just talking about how things are going. You are usually ending or beginning a new beat, and meaningful physical action is something of a prerequisite. As the writer you make this happen first in the script, with the anticipation that the director will fully capitalize on it.

The moment ending the mid-point crisis should complicate your drama and your protagonist's goal. What new obstacles might it present that could threaten your main character's objective?

If the character is on the run and reactive, this is often the point where she stops running and turns and faces her adversaries. Hedda finds out that Tesman has come up with Løvborg's cherished manuscript: what is she going to do with it? Oedipus begins to think that he might be the guilty one: is he still going to pursue the investigation now or shut it down? What is the elemental question that your main character faces at this point in the story? Does this crisis involve a change in direction, such as a stronger commitment to accomplishing his goal? Is this the point of no return—no going back at this point—because he has burned his bridges? It could be the point where the main character thinks he has solved the problem, but we know better. Does he come up with a new plan?

Act Two continues at a blistering pace. There are more ups and downs for your protagonist. Look again at your character arc and be sure that you are challenging your characters at all levels of interaction (the egocentric, the interactive, and the environmental or contextual). It often takes all three to sustain progressive complication through your Act Two journey. In *Brendan's Journey* (1997), Brendan is sailing the Atlantic. Personally, he is beginning to go mad. In addition, his relationship with Birt, his half-brother, is deteriorating. Environmentally, he is contending with the ocean and the elements themselves. Near the end your protagonist might look like he is going to win the day for his side. But his own failings, the ascendency of the antagonist, betrayals, obstacles all combine to challenge his progress, all of which leads to your Act Two climax.

## Act Two Climax

Your Act Two climactic scene usually happens after your progressive complication has brought your protagonist to the lowest point of experience. It happens about three-quarters of the way through the play.

The protagonist has not been able to overcome her flaw yet, and it looks like she might not be able to. Plot development has resulted in putting her in a position whereby it seems like she will not accomplish her goal. But circumstances arise whereby she can somehow overcome the obstacles that are beating her down. She is not saved by others, but often by her own resources. She finds a strategy and renewed direction.

Literally, your Act Two climax serves as a crisis for your Act Three climax, which often results in your protagonist realizing her potential, facing her limitations and transcending them, and starting to find a new vision, a new meaning, and new powers. Your Act Two climax is when the subplot characters surrounding your protagonist slough off, desert your hero, so she is left on her own. It is often a point where your character seeks out higher, more spiritual, even transcendent solutions. She is now up to facing her greatest fear, though it is usually left to the Act Three climax for her to defeat this fear. Christ's Act Two climax is the Garden Gethsemane (Matt. 26:36–46) and the crucifixion (27:32–56). Deserted. Crying out to God. Under great physical torment, Christ's Act Three climax is "He is risen indeed" (See Matt. 28).

By this time, you have become good at exploring the "What Ifs" or possible permutations and combinations of plot machinations that are lined up against your central character. Ask yourself, "what is the worst thing that can happen to my character?"—then make it worse. This is the "all is lost" moment. In romantic comedy, it is the "guy loses girl" moment, or vice versa. In tragedy, it is the hero's realization that he has blown it. In *King Lear* (c. 1606), Lear is driven mad with the loss of identity as a King and father. Othello (c. 1604) is sure that Desdemona has betrayed him. Hamlet returns from his sea journey knowing that he is going to die. It is the moment when the hero questions his quest, when he doubts his resources, when he is physically compromised, and when he doubts God himself. It is a moment when your central character can express anger, hurt, culpability, despair, and evidence with a bit more vulnerability than he has in the past. It is also a moment when the audience can identify more personally with your character's plight. Perhaps it is also the moment when the character's greatest fear looks like it has triumphed and he begins to realize that his flaw is what is doing him in. It is also a time when someone with some insight, a mentor or guide in some way, will offer her hard advice to take. Whatever the problem, she still must find the resources within and around herself to begin the process of renewal and awakening that will provide the fortitude to proceed to the final climax in Act Three.

The paradox can be found in the realization that as negative the situation is, it is often just what the main character needs to finally face what is pursuing him both internally and externally, and to let go of what is propping him up and to bring about the much-needed change. He can no longer run, he can no longer be in denial, he must face and confront what he is and what he has been running from.

So now armed with the truth about himself and his situation, he is equipped to pursue the quest to the battle at the end. How is this accomplished? The ending does not have to be victorious for it to be complete or ultimately satisfying. If he does fail, at least now he has hopefully developed the foresight to know that what he has sacrificed for has ultimate meaning and worth. He might not have accomplished his goal, but he has provided us with a symbol of how to go down in glory, or how to pass on the baton. For instance, Lear is stripped of everything, but as he spends his last breath holding Cordelia, he has found the ultimate meaning of who he is—no longer King but as father/child to his daughter. His friends watch as his spirit ascends to heaven.

## Act Three Climax

Equipped with new resolve, with new strategies, perhaps, the protagonist has a clearer concept of what is wanted and what is needed. She has a renewed sense of dedication toward serving the good, in establishing a new order, and in somehow returning to the community more than what she left with. The protagonist now ventures into the final battle, the final confrontation, the final testing of her will against the forces arrayed against her.

Of course, every Act Three climax is not composed of all these elements, but they represent a bold array of at least some of the physical and moral elements which can be overcome. These are all triumphant expressions of a successful and meaningful journey by the central character. If he falls short or misses the mark, if the moment passes him by, or if he is unable to grab the prize—e.g., get the girl, overcome his flaw, or have a new perspective on the meaning of life—then all we can hope for is that he sees and understands his failure.

Consider Arthur Miller's *Death of a Salesman*. Willy Loman commits suicide at the recognition of his failure as a father, salesman, and husband. If we see our own failings in Willy and are motivated to change them, then the identification factor that Miller has sought is successful. Or Hedda Gabler, who shoots herself in the head when she realizes that all she has sought to possess and to rule over has been destroyed or has eluded her, and her one recourse is not to become a slave to a culture and to relationships which she abhors. Her escape is a cowardly one.

Additionally, Judas's betrayal of Jesus (Matt. 26:14–15) precipitates an unchangeable series of events that lead to the death of Jesus—absolute good—and at the same time foreshadows an ultimate victory that he is unable to celebrate. The servant figure of Grusha in Bertolt Brecht's *The Caucasian Chalk Circle* perseveres against the highest and corrupt forces in the kingdom and is allowed to keep the young Prince that she rescued and risked all to save and succor. And Portia in *The Merchant of Venice* (c. 1598), masking as a lawyer in a courtroom scene that could easily end in immolation, through brazen reason and God-inspired moral reckoning brings about justice against the retributive declarations of Shylock. She triumphs as a woman in a courtroom of men. She assures that her fiancé's best friend, Antonio, will not be killed, and she establishes a new criterion for mercy rather than revenge, upholding the very standard of God's revelation to us in Scripture. In other words, the ending is worked out at the three levels of personal, interpersonal, and extra-personal criteria.

In some plays such as *Doubt: A Parable* (2004), by John Patrick Shanley, which is a parable examining the questionable power of accusation and of unqualified judgement, we wonder at the guilt or innocence of Father Flynn in terms of his having sexual relationships with a boy student. In the end Sister Aloysius, who is unwavering in her condemnation of the priest, expresses doubts surrounding the allegations. It is the antagonist here who has the "ah-ha" realization that she might have been culpable of rigid moralizing, and that she should have honored or at least explored more fully her inner feelings of doubt.

In the play version of *To Kill a Mockingbird* (2018), Tom Robinson is wrongly convicted by a White jury, but at the same time the lawyer Atticus brilliantly exposes the racial bigotry that rules in this small Alabama town in 1936. We do not get legal justice, but we become more aware of moral justice. So the Act Three climax does not always guarantee success or change or popularity and acceptance of the central character's final working out of his quest or journey. But the insight or revelation gained by the audience should encourage them to ponder the truths and contradictions of how we live together as human beings. If the Act Three climax does not offer us anything that we can learn from, and perhaps better our own lives as we look deeper into ourselves and our relationships and our work, then its ultimate worth must be questioned. It is in this area that the theme is worked out through action and deemed worthy or not. Structurally, the components of what constitutes a good Act Three climax are noted in the following questions:

- Is the essential question that was posed at the point of attack addressed in the Act Three climax satisfactorily? Is your Act Three climax the obligatory scene, the necessary scene, to the realization and proving of your point of attack? The main question could have become more complex and even changed some, but how has it been answered in some way? Sometimes, remember, that the question is answered by addressing your main character's unconscious desire rather than his conscious desire. So for example, he does not get the job he was seeking but he finds the family he needs.

- Is your protagonist brought together in a final confrontation with your antagonist? Are personalities and physical bodies in conflict, as well as their varied value systems? The Act Three climax must be related to the Act Two climax, and we must believe that the central character has been equipped with enough personal and professional resources to be able to rise above the vicissitudes of his Act Two climactic challenges. At this point there should not be any accidents or coincidences. This final testing ground has been meticulously cultivated with motivational events and relationships throughout the entire play/story that ring true, that are possible, and that have some sort of worth or meaning. Having the cavalry arrive just in time to save the day is the stuff of melodrama.

- Does the Act Three climax involve a decision of some sort in which the very core of the protagonist is tested to determine if she indeed is up to the challenge presented? The plot progression at this point must create the matrix of events so the hero *has* to make a decision.

- Does the Act Three climax confront the central character with his flaw and make him face it and hopefully be able to overcome it?

- Does the Act Three climax confront the central character with her greatest fear?

- Is there a plot twist which presents us with a surprise? What new twist or turn can you throw at the main character that he did not anticipate? Does this new revelation, a secret perhaps or a deeper realization, provide your central character with some of the means to continue to pursue her objective? What about a reversal, in which you lead the character to expect one thing but provide her, and us, the audience, with something we had not thought about?

- How do you draw attention to the Act Three climax? The Act Three climax is not talked about or stated. It is enacted.

- Your subplots are almost always affected and brought to closure because of this climactic moment. How is this done in your final climactic scene?

- What is the culminating image? Do you have a single image that the audience will remember the play by in your Act Three climax? It is sometimes harder to create the powerful visual imagery on the stage than in film. But I believe it is the writer's challenge to create such a picture. King Lear, for instance, holding Cordelia at the end of the play says it all. *Peer Gynt*, peeling an onion and finding nothing at its core tells the story of his life's journey.

- How are your characters transformed in terms of inner thought life, in terms of relationships, and in terms of their relation to the community or their cultural context? Often a new order is established at the end of your Act Three climactic scene or in the ending. Does your play establish a new order in these terms?

- What elements of redemption can you reveal in this final climactic action? Perhaps your character now realizes that the working out of their story has been one of personal destiny fulfilled. Perhaps they have acquired an element of hope that goes beyond good luck or coincidence. Perhaps they now realize they could not have done it by themselves alone, that something more was needed, that they are not totally sufficient unto themselves. Could they have experienced a mystery, something that they cannot explain but that makes them wonder about the deeper questions of why life is the way it is?

## The Denouement

The *denouement* can be defined as the final disentangling of the intricacies of a plot, after the story's climax is played out. Or, more technically, it is all the scenes that come after the final battle is engaged in the Act Three climax. It provides a cooling off period. The dust is settling and there is time provided for the main characters to look at where they have been and what it has meant, and to ponder the future. Oftentimes, subplots are brought to closure here. The denouement is also the beginning of a new balance or order. The ruptures caused by the Act Three climax have subsided and things are hopefully looking up. Perhaps justice has now prevailed; a new moral order is established; marriages are resolved or now take place; evil has been vanquished, at least for a time.

The denouement is also the place where the main character now realizes that his unconscious goal has become conscious and is functioning not as desire but as realization. Finally, since it is the last chapter of your full-length play, it can be changed at will so do not worry about getting it right on the first draft. It can change, and perhaps will, as your awareness of the direction of your Act Three climax is revealed and as your subplots change. I like to think of the thousand-year millennium and the coming of the City of God or New Jerusalem as the denouement of Scripture. It follows a horrendous Act Three climax comprised of Armageddon and the plagues, wars, and natural disasters of the Tribulation. It brings forth and establishes a new king, a new government, and an entirely new relationship between God and the nations. The rewards are personal salvation. There is still work to be done, but it will be done differently now. The enemy has been vanquished from earth and from our hearts. Even the placement and function of the cosmos could be altered.

## Framing Devices

You have the given of the stage, which usually is a square box that begins as a neutral playing space. The *proscenium*, or the part of the theater in front of the curtain, or any theater space is a natural framing device. It can be transformed into anything you want. By making choices and delimiting the possibilities of that space you can increase the theatricality and unity of the play.

But other kinds of framing devices can be used by writers to facilitate a way of getting into and out of the play. They can provide the audience with a touchstone about place and action that carries the plot visually and often narratively. They can be created by a character, by a set piece or visual design, and can be identified through the usage of a narrator. Several examples of framing devices are included below:

- **The Narrator**. The narrator, if used, should be organic to the show, meaning that if he or she has an investment, even plays a part in it, all the better. The character of Tom in Tennessee Williams' *The Glass Menagerie* (1944) functions in this capacity. Also, the Narrator in *Our Town* (1938), who serves as commentator, introducing us to character and situation, and, in character, even to the meaning of the play.

- **Transformational Set**. William Shakespeare's *The Taming of the Shrew* (c. 1592) is actually a play within a play, as the Lord's attendants produce the *Shrew* play for a drunken Tinker named Sly. In a production of *Cabaret* (1966) that I directed, the Kit Kat Club was introduced in the opening musical number and as a functional set never left the stage. Large platforms rolled on with the other interior sets on them, right into the club itself. This technique was also used in *Five Cups of Coffee* (2006) in which all the action was played in or in front of Milo's Gourmet Coffee Shop, even though we travel through time and space throughout the drama.

- **Alternative Entertainment Devices**. For example, the changing environments of *Brendan's Journey* are framed by the characters presenting a travelogue slide show. *Everywoman* (2013) also uses a television talk show set as a backdrop for the action. I directed a production of Christopher Marlowe's *Dr. Faustus* (1592) that was set against the backdrop of a traveling 1920s caravan side show in the dust bowl. The play of *Hamlet* in Tom Stoppard's *Rosencrantz and Guildenstern are Dead* (1966) forms the backdrop for this existential comedy with the actors being unable to escape the destiny of being caught in a tragedy. The music hall in John Osborne's *The Entertainer* (1957) is also a much-used context for the dramatic action which features an ageing music hall entertainer. A similar image is used in terms of frantic action via a music hall feel in Peter Nichol's *A Day in the Life of Joe Egg* (1967).

- **A Functional Workplace**. As an action it can be seen in *The Contractor* (1970), David Storey's play, in which the actors build and take down a wedding tent.

The framing device is sometimes a director's ploy rather than a writer's ploy, but why should it be? If you can imagine a functional and artistically challenging and thematically appropriate framing device for your play, structure it into the script—it will make a difference and enhance the entire creative usage of the theater conventions. For instance, the Apostle John, as an old man, could introduce and comment on a play version of Revelation from his cave dwelling on the island of Patmos (see Rev. 1:9). I wrote a version of the story of Rahab, in which she tells and enacts her story to a group of children that she is overseeing after joining God's people in the Promised land.

## Discussion Questions and Exercises

1. Exposition is the beginning of your play. Using the first ten pages of a play you are working on, have written, or a play of your own choosing, answer the following questions.

   - In the first ten pages, what questions are you raising in the audience's mind?

   - Are any of your main characters introduced or at least have you set it up that we are anticipating their entrance?

   - What sort of expository devices are you using? Conflict. Humor.

Narrator. Emotion. Remember, you are introducing important backstory elements in the story.

- How are you utilizing the physical context to ground your first ten pages? Context implies an environment with people doing something. For example, mom is making lunch for her child before he goes to school. Why is this important and relevant?

2. Point of Attack. The major inciting incident, or point of attack, is the scene where the action that defines the premise first coalesces. It defines the characters' main objective. It is the beginning of the point of no return for your protagonist, in which he is confronted with a problem and has to take action. Oftentimes that action can be found in the Act One climax. Find the point of attack in your play and note how it satisfies the criteria provided above.

3. Mid-point Crisis. Your mid-point crisis usually happens just before your intermission. Come up with three or more reasons why the audience is compelled to come back after intermission and see the second half of your play idea.

4. Act Two Complication. You know your protagonist and her goal. Brainstorm possibilities of what might happen to your hero. Do not interrupt your creative flow by judging whether it is a good or bad idea. Apply this to your treatment. Even if you have written your Act Two, apply this exercise to see where you can charge it up with more complications. Think of conflict in terms of action, but also in terms of subplot developments with secondary characters.

5. Act Two Climax. Ask yourself, "what is the worst thing that can happen to my character?"—then make it worse. This is the "all is lost" moment. It is the moment when the hero questions his quest, when he doubts his resources, when he is physically compromised, when he doubts God himself. Whatever the problem, he still must find the resources within and around himself to begin the process of renewal and awakening that will provide the fortitude to beat this and proceed to the final climax in Act Three. Describe your Act Two climax in terms of reflecting the above criteria.

6. Act Three Climax. In this chapter is a list of questions dealing with what the Act Three climax is supposed to accomplish. Apply these to your Act Three climax as it exists in either treatment or play format.

# Chapter 11

# The Synopsis and the Treatment

THE *SYNOPSIS* AND THE TREATMENT are both outlining and organizational tools created by the playwright which serve as structural guidelines in creating a workable shape and function to your drama. They can also be used to serve as an overview of your work in terms of disseminating your idea to publishers, agents, and theater producing organizations. A synopsis, written in a lively manner, can sell the idea of your script from a basic story standpoint.

## The Synopsis

The following should be included in and addressed by your synopsis:

- A title of the work.
- A story outline not to exceed three pages, single spaced, and which includes plot points. (Note: for a commercial synopsis all the plot points need not be labeled, but unlike the premise or log line the final conflict and resolution should be included.)
- An introduction to the main character and his objectives as well as the antagonist character or force. This should provide the author with the idea of the theme without it being stated.
- It should establish what the main conflict is.
- It should begin at the point of the very opening of the play.
- It should include the names of the main characters.
- It should be written with a consciousness of the power of active verbs.

You do not need to do the following in writing a synopsis:

- Do not feel the need to provide a lot of backstory.
- Do not spend time explaining or justifying why you are writing the story that you are.

- Do not present the theme as a theme, but as something that arises out of the action.

The following is an example of a plot point synopsis for Ibsen's play *Hedda Gabler* (1891):

**Set Up**: Hedda, the daughter of an aristocratic and enigmatic general, has just returned to her villa in Kristiania (now Oslo) from her honeymoon. Her husband is George Tesman, a young, aspiring, and reliable (but not brilliant) academic who continued his research during their honeymoon. It becomes clear in the play that she has never loved him but married him because she thinks her years of youthful abandon are over. It is also suggested that she may be pregnant.

**Inciting Incident**: The reappearance of George's academic rival, Eilert Løvborg, throws their lives into disarray. Eilert, a writer, is also a recovered alcoholic who has wasted his talent until now. Thanks to a relationship with Hedda's old schoolmate, Thea Elvsted (who has left her husband for him), Løvborg shows signs of rehabilitation and has just published a bestseller in the same field as George. When Hedda and Eilert talk privately together, it becomes apparent that they are former lovers.

**Act One Climax**: The critical success of his recently published work makes Eilert a threat to George, as Eilert is now a competitor for the university professorship George had been counting on. George and Hedda are financially overstretched, and George tells Hedda that he will not be able to finance the regular entertaining or luxurious housekeeping that she had been expecting. Upon meeting Eilert, however, the couple discover that he has no intention of competing for the professorship, but rather has spent the last few years laboring with Thea over what he considers to be his masterpiece, the "sequel" to his recently published work.

**Mid-point Crisis** (About halfway through Act Two): Apparently jealous of Thea's influence over Eilert, Hedda hopes to come between them. Despite his drinking problem, she encourages Eilert to accompany George and his associate, Judge Brack, to a party. George returns home from the party and reveals that he found the complete manuscript of Eilert's great work, which the latter lost while drunk. What will Hedda do now?

**Intermission**

**Act Two Crisis**: When Eilert next sees Hedda, he confesses to her, despairingly, that he has lost the manuscript. Instead of telling him that the manuscript has been found, Hedda encourages him to commit suicide, giving him a pistol. She then burns the manuscript and tells George she has destroyed it to secure their future.

**Act Two Climax**: When the news comes that Eilert has indeed killed himself, George and Thea are determined to try to reconstruct his book from Eilert's notes, which Thea has kept. Hedda is shocked to discover from Judge Brack that Eilert's death, in a brothel, was messy and probably accidental; this "ridiculous and vile" death contrasts with the "beautiful and free" one that Hedda had imagined for him.

**Act Three Climax**: Worse, Brack knows the origins of the pistol. He tells Hedda that if he reveals what he knows, a scandal will likely arise around her. Hedda realizes that this places Brack in a position of power over her. Leaving the others, she goes into her smaller room and shoots herself in the head. The others in the room assume that Hedda is simply firing shots, and they follow the sound to investigate. The play ends with George, Brack, and Thea discovering her body.

Additional plot points, reversals, and complications can be utilized in the plot but not every one of these needs to be delineated in the synopsis.

## The Treatment

The *treatment* is a lengthy document which records the action of your play in a scene-by-scene manner. It is the first copyrightable document that you create—that is, ideas and synopses cannot be copyrighted. The treatment focuses the story on an event-by-event basis while at the same time providing an overview of the bigger picture. It should be written in a user-friendly and dramatic style using highly visual prose, always in the present tense, and highlights, in broad strokes, your story's primary characters, conflicts, and themes.

## Key Elements of the Treatment

The following should be included in and addressed by your treatment:

- Brevity. It should be anywhere from twelve to twenty-five pages. It should be easy on the eye, written in paragraph form, and single spaced.

- Genre, title, set. Establish the genre, the title, and describe the set.

- Action description. You want the reader to visualize the story, so write graphically because it is supposed to capture the imagination of the reader in describing the sequential evolution of the plot action.

- Constant change. It is used by you as a structural tool as you write the play. But it is not written in concrete.

- Backstory. Do not try and fill in the backstory elements. The story should stand by itself. It should include the necessary details for the story to be understood. Do not write story digressions as clever as they might seem.

- Dialogue. Dialogue should be used sparingly. Include snippets or phrases which you have fallen in love with and think truly typify character.

- Action. You are writing action that is happening now. Do not write "the story starts with" or "in this scene we see." Never use the royal "we."

- Main characters and primary subplots. Introduce all the main characters and primary subplots. You are writing conflict, turning points, and changes in direction or "twists" which need to be included and featured. A *twist* is an unexpected turning point that surprises the audience. These propel readers from one Act to another. These include your crisis and climax points which are also your plot points. The following should be labeled in your treatment in addition to reversals and turning points that are not listed under the following:

  » Balance or imbalance
  » Inciting incident
  » Act One climax
  » Mid-point crisis

» Intermission
» Act Two climax
» Act Three climax
» Denouement

## Treatment Examples

An example of the kind of detailed writing you do for a treatment to describe a scene is provided below. Hopefully your play will be composed of about twelve to twenty events: i.e., significant changes in direction, surprises, climaxes, crises, and reversals that complicate the plot and move your story forward.

Have you set up the circumstances so that the revelatory scene/event must happen now? If a scene of this nature happens too early, then you have nowhere to go. If it happens too late, then it feels contrived, like a playwright's ploy. For example, a mother knows that her son, Stephen, is not the marrying kind, and she gets along beautifully with him, hiding behind that phrase, not facing the reality of the choices that he has made. When he insists on telling her that he hopes to marry Jake and that Jake is out in the car and he wants her to meet him, she asks her son to leave and never talks to him again.

- Two objectives: Stephen, to tell his mom about his relationship. Mom, to fight to stay as a mom to Stephen, her child, and to shelter herself and him from any adult interferences.

- Secrets: Stephen—he is gay. Mom—her brother, Stephen's Uncle Albert, the unnamed one, whom he has never met, came out as gay years before and she blames him for destroying her childhood.

- Why now? Stephen is getting married. His partner, Jake, is insisting that all be let out and be known.

Scene coverage in a Treatment:

SCENE THREE: MOTHER'S LIVING ROOM

STEPHEN enters with flowers. His MOTHER smothers him with memories.

He says that he has found the right person.

She talks about how she fell in love with Stephen's father, about how she knew that he would be the proper man of the family even before she married him.

Stephen asks about Uncle Albert, her brother.

She doesn't know any Uncle Albert.

He denies this. Produces a letter . . .

//

She shows him a picture album of her and her brothers and sisters— no Uncle Albert, she laughs it off.

He starts to read the letter.

She tells him that couldn't be—that Uncle Albert is dead.

//

She goes to the window— wishes the children were home to rake the leaves.

He points out the car to her. With Jake sitting in it.

She insists that he invite Jake in.

Stephen tells her they are soon to be married.

// CONFUSION!

She talks about how she always pictured him getting married. About that Simpson girl down the street, who would be so perfect . . .

//

He starts for the door to get Jake.

She turns on him.

She talks about things proper—being proper, that's all she ever asked of him. There are certain things not said, certain things not discussed.

He says it's time they talked about "things."

She knew something was wrong when she thought he was going to Mrs. McKinney's dancing lessons.

"When I was really hiding in the bushes," he says.

She tells him that she knows things are difficult and that if he would like, since Julie has moved away, that there is an extra bedroom upstairs, that he could move in. She would take care of him.

He tells her that he has found someone else to live with, for the rest of his life. He tells her that all her life she has avoided anything that she doesn't see as "in its place." He accuses her of being behind the times. Of being blind.

//

Full of invective she tells him about her brother, his Uncle Albert. The hate that pours forth overwhelms him. Silence.

She regroups and tells him that it would be fine if he left now, after all, everyone is leaving, aren't they?

The car honks.

//

He tells her that he must go.

She tells him that certain lines have been crossed. Things have been said that can't be taken back. She doesn't ever want to see him again.

He sits in a chair and cries.

She, humming to herself, looks at the pictures in the album.

He leaves.//

Another example of a treatment is provided below from the play *Everywoman* (2013), which is based very loosely on *Everyman*, the fifteenth-century medieval morality play. It is futuristic.

The SET is a television talk show environment, a couple of swivel chairs, a low table between them, media background with one or more Screens, all slightly elevated. Downstage of the set is an open playing area where the action can move just about any place.

The television set can revolve, and Eve's apartment appears on the other side.

EVE, the protagonist and everywoman, is a talk show host. She is in her thirties, attractive, glib.

## ACT ONE: Stage of Grief—Denial

### Scene One: On the Road

EVE (37) is standing over a roadkill. She has a microphone in her hand. DANNY is filming her with a digital camera which can be projected on the screen. At her feet is a roadkill. She is lamenting the death of innocence, of creatures who are victims of our technology: birds and jet planes and those huge windmill killers and salmon trying to swim upstream through suction lifts and goldfish which get flushed down the toilet bowl.

### Inciting Incident: Death Makes His Entrance on a Motorcycle.

DEATH tells her it's "time." She tries to worm her way out. There must be some mistake. He tells her to get on his hog. DANNY cannot see DEATH. No way out. DEATH rides off. She tries a cell phone, and nobody answers. She is outside of time and space. Maybe DANNY is frozen or going about his business and is not noticed. She tries walking and then running away. Sound effect. Time stops. While the actor playing Death gets into place as the Policeman. She is frozen.

### Scene Two: At the Police Station

She is complaining about being stalked by Death, at least that is what he says his name is. He rides a hog and wears a Prussian helmet and has tattoos of . . . Dragons. He also looks scorched. Nothing wrong. No violence. She is a personality, a well-known personality. She runs a talk show on a local station. People know her. The POLICEMAN promises to keep an eye out. She wants protection. He cannot offer it. Things are not going well. Food shipments aren't going into town. The Cop is eating donuts galore.

*(And so, it proceeds on from scene to scene and Act to Act.)*

The treatment is designed to serve as a memory device to remind you of the placement and progression of your central action and your subplots. It also allows you to step back and look at the evolving form of your drama and to sense what is not working and what needs attention. Some of the red flags which a treatment can raise are suggested below:

- You do not know your characters well enough. What are they hiding and why? What do they hide behind: sarcasm, fear of confrontation, jokes, self-deprecation, bluster, or threats? What are their innermost fears? What incidents in their past have made them the way that they are? In other words, what are your characters' secrets and what does it take to get them out in the open? It should never be easy. You do not have to just know these things; you must know why and how your characters manifest them through action and dialogue. What are the personal idiosyncrasies of behavior?

- You are not sure of your characters' objectives. If you are not sure, then your characters are not sure. In every scene try listing the obstacles that your character faces in achieving her objective—conscious and unconscious. Also, every character in a scene should have an objective. If you have just one character with an objective, then the others become pawns to the playwright, and usually the conflict in the scene suffers.

- As noted earlier, the circumstances you set forth do not make it the absolute right time for the revelatory scene to happen. If a revelatory scene happens too early, then you have nowhere to go. If it happens too late, then it feels contrived, a playwright's ploy.

## Discussion Questions and Exercises

1. The synopsis. Questions to answer as you write this three-page, single spaced document.

   - Is there a cause-and-effect relationship within the plot development of my story? Are their enough events to warrant this being a full-length piece?

   - Is there the germ idea for subplots? Are the characters complicated enough to deserve them?

   - Is the story worth telling?

   - Is there a reversal or a change of direction for my main character/characters? Do you sense a character arc?

   - Who or what is my antagonist?

   - Is there an effective climax that meaningfully completes the action and addresses the problem poised in the point of attack?

2. The treatment. The major problems that are too often evident in the creation of a treatment for the stage play are as follows:

- Do not describe what the characters are thinking, their internal monologues, unless they are spoken out loud on stage. Is your treatment designed to depict action, what people do?

- Are the beat changes evident and scored in your treatment?

- Is your treatment dialogue heavy? How can you describe what is going on narratively rather than with dialogue?

# Chapter 12

# Subplots

WHAT IS A *SUBPLOT*? Literally, it is everything that happens around the plot that features the lives and concerns of secondary characters. It can also be another venue that your central character might be involved with. But it usually involves other characters who should have histories, worries, and objectives of their own, and whose concerns are either directly or tangentially related to the overriding concerns of the central character. Finding effective subplot relationships in a two-hander play is often difficult. You can create imaginary characters who they interface with; you can also provide characters who they talk with on the phone, or text, or perhaps they have a favorite doll or picture or image that they treat like a character.

Technically, subplots function to provide different perspectives, points of view, and cultural standards that the main character does not necessarily possess. They are often designed to present new conflicting elements into your story, add color and variety of characterization, and serve as romantic counterparts to the main character's interpersonal relationships. They can be used as expositional providers to provide new information into the story that would not be organic for the central character to dwell on. They can also provide varying moral perspectives on behavior that challenge and highlight the central character's worldview.

Oftentimes when writing overt Christian characters, playwrights resort to secondary characters to represent the more traditional faith values. But remember that your subplot characters should have their own objectives, their own backstory, and their own desperation. They are often noted as SUBPLOT A, B, C, D, and so on, when recorded in the treatment. Multi-protagonist stories/scripts often are a blending of several subplot stories into one meaningful whole, such as in *Moonchildren* (1971), originally titled *Cancer*, a play by Brooklyn-based playwright Michael Weller. The play chronicles a year-in-the-life of the "moonchildren" referred to in the title: eight college students living communally together in an off-campus attic in the mid-1960s.

Intersect your subplot with the main story plot and allow this subplot to create new complications for your protagonist. Subplots can run parallel to the main storyline, or they can run in complete contrast to it, but all subplots should support, inform, and eventually wrap up or pay off into your main story plot.

The climax for the subplot often happens right before, during, or right after the Act Three climax. They can set us up or they can help us to understand the implications of the actions of the main climax. Examples of and additional insights about subplots are provided below:

- Subplots are used to throw additional light on the protagonist(s)—to experience him or her from different perspectives. In Hamlet's relationship with Ophelia, we see elements of emotion and madness not displayed in other places or with other characters. Interestingly, most romantic affairs are often revealed as subplot phenomenon. Hedda Gabler's relationship with her husband Tesman, and his personal relationship with Thea (subplot), provides justification for her impatience and dominance over men. Or consider Tom's relationship with Jim (subplot), the gentleman caller in *The Glass Menagerie* (1944)—Tom just seems to shut up when Jim intrudes into the family, and he is the kind of character who offers a masculine extroversion to Jim's reticence. And Ruth brings out Lenny's insecurities in Harold Pinter's *The Homecoming* (1965). In Scripture, Joseph's relationship with Potiphar's wife is a subplot that ends up putting him in jail, but it is important, because it is from jail that he is able to gain the audience of the Pharoah of Egypt (see Gen. 39).

- Subplots are used to juxtapose opposites with the protagonist. For example, Kate's tempestuousness with her sister Bianca's feminine coyness in *The Taming of the Shrew* (c. 1590). Another good example is Eben as the passionate lover as opposed to the dominate brutality of his father in Eben's relationships with Abbie in *Desire Under the Elms* (1924). And the mad but noble Don Quixote is balanced by Sancho Panza, the practical low life servant who also offers comic relief in *Man from La Mancha* (1965).

- Subplots are used to connect protagonists to other cultural worlds. *The King and I* (1951) juxtaposes Anna, the western teacher, with the King of Siam. John Book, tough Philly cop, goes to live with the Amish in the *The Witness*, and his attraction to Rachel is part of the subplot as is her relationship to the Amish farmer, Daniel. Consider

Marco Polo, the crass Western tradesman, who is a counterbalance to Kublai Khan, the noble idealistic Asian ruler in Eugene O'Neill's *Marco's Millions* (1923), and is in subplot relationship with his daughter, Princess Kukachin. And in *A Streetcar Named Desire* (1947), there could not be more different characters than Blanche, the educated Southern lady, and Mitch, the uneducated working guy.

- Subplots are often the romantic entanglements that the protagonist gets into. These can sometimes turn into main plots. Starbuck and Lizzie in Richard Nash's *The Rainmaker* (1954) form a love relationship in the middle of a drought. John Book and Rachel in *The Witness* form a subplot to the corrupt police murder main plot. These are often more character than plot driven. Look for an emotional context. C. S. Lewis in the film *Shadowlands* (1989) and his relationship with Joy's son is a good example.

- Subplots can offer humorous or comic secondary characters. For instance, the Pigeon sisters in *The Odd Couple* (1965), who primarily show us how far these two guys are from finding love outside of marriage. Or Shakespeare's Malvolio and Andrew Aguecheek in *Twelfth Night* (c. 1602), who both represent comic parallels to Puritanism and mindless aristocratic manners respectively. In addition, their fumbling comic romantic endeavors are contrasted with the more authentic love relationship between Orsino and Viola.

- Subplots are used to complicate the action. They make things harder on the protagonist.

- Subplots have their own climaxes and happen both during the Act Three climax and sometimes before and after. The "before" and "after" are there to sustain suspense in terms of the greater revelation of Act Three.

## Discussion Questions and Exercises

1. Identify as many subplots in one of your favorite playscripts and note how they accomplish any or all of the usages that this chapter identifies. Remember, subplots are always connected with another character who is in some relationship with the protagonist.

2. Identify the subplots in your play idea. Consider any or all of the following:

- How are subplots used to juxtapose opposites with your protagonist in terms of personality characteristics?

- How do subplots serve as romantic entanglements?

- How do subplots cause conflict and create obstacles to the protagonist's objective or goal?

3. Subplots have climaxes of their own or are integrated into the protagonist's Act Three climax. Identify where each of your subplots have their final climax in your overall script idea and note how they function in terms of reflecting a pro or con stance in terms of the protagonist establishing her overall goal.

# Chapter 13

# Theme

WHY YOU ARE WRITING YOUR PLAY finds the most meaningful expression in the *theme* or controlling idea you are trying to communicate; it should consist of something that you personally believe to be important and even life changing. These themes can encompass a wide range of considerations, from interpersonal relationships to something more political or polemical (ideological) in nature. Noting what vitally concerns you in terms of the human condition is a good place to start.

If I were to make a list of personal preoccupations, I think it would start with why we were created or what our purpose is as conscious beings made in God's image. I am also fascinated with how a so-called first world country like Germany could sink to the barbarous state that it did in World War II, and how close we are as individuals to being able to do the same? I perpetually wonder about how we live in two worlds at once, the material world of present-day cognizance and a spiritual world that is outside time and space as we normally relate to it. What destines a person for hell, and how do we create that hell for ourselves during this short lifetime? I am interested in the idea of sacrifice, of giving oneself up for another person or a community because you believe so intensely in something that you would die for it. I am also interested in personal integrity, and how we play games with ourselves and with God by deceiving ourselves about who we are and denying that He knows us to the core of our being. Can anyone live with the knowledge that we share every bit of our person with another—and a supreme being at that?

Of course, what themes occupy your imagination are unique to you and that is how it should be. We should be challenging both the dominant culture and our marginalized Christian subculture in multiple ways—ways that provoke, satirize, encourage, and advocate that there is hope, and put forth a view of existence that says, "life can be better in some ways than it might seem."

It has been noted that there are only so many themes that can be recorded in fiction. One book by Georges Polti puts the number at around thirty-five.[1] So the challenge is not worrying about articulating something that is totally original but in creating a new perspective on an established theme. Themes can be categorized using such terms as revenge, betrayal, or jealousy. For example, *Cinderella* (1957) and *Pygmalion* (1912) are essentially the story of a poor outcast being recognized for valuable traits and going through a radical change. So the theme is summed up in the action.

Below are a variety of themes that might be found in things like aphorisms, Aesop's Fables, generic proverbs, and more:

- A bad workman always blames his tools.
- A burnt child dreads the fire.
- Actions speak louder than words.
- A fault confessed is half redressed.
- All is well that ends well.
- All that glitters is not gold.
- All work and no play makes Jack a dull boy.
- An ounce of prevention is worth a pound of cure.
- As you sow so shall you reap.
- Better to be alone than in bad company.
- Better safe than sorry.
- Better to get an egg a day than a hen tomorrow.
- Bird in hand is worth two in the bush.
- Cheaters never prosper.
- Despair gives courage to a coward.

In *God's Story Structure*, Michael Torres writes the following to put forth his specific thematic approach to writing for the Christian:

> For if the Christian writer is not in the least communicating to draw the audience to some degree or another to a crisis of belief, then for what purpose does the Christian writer communicate? That crisis of belief does not have to ultimately come to (or culminate in) the crisis of "eternal salvation" in every work produced but the Christian writer in every work should at least indicate the transformation from a condition of humanity that is degenerative, fostering sin/death to some degree or another, to a condition of humanity that is generative, or representative of the

Life of Christ. This can be as simple as the acknowledgment of the destructive nature of anger in relationships and the triumph to a marked, discernible measure over that anger. It can also be communicated as the total transformation of a life hell-bent on destroying any concept of God to one that is humbled and acknowledges the existence of this sin existence and seeks to find hope in what we would term God's light.[2]

How does the idea of a theme evolve? An example is provided in the following: you see an action. A woman on the streets of Beirut is carrying her dead child, trying to nurse it. Your first reaction is confusion, how can you help, you are dodging bullets! But you cannot get the image out of your head. You begin to structure the images. You begin to create a story for the woman and the child. An idea emerges: what war can be justified when it entails the death of the innocent?

If you begin your writing by saying to yourself, "I'm going to write a play about . . .", then you could end up putting theme before story in terms of characterization and action and beating your audience over the head with it. Theme is often something that you have carried around with you for a long time. It can come from imagery, from a gesture, from an incident, event, or even a word. If you discover halfway through your story that your theme has eluded you, then do not worry about it. Keep writing. Your sub-conscious is doing the work. It will emerge, though it could surprise you in how it might change as you create the story.

Below are listed some of the important technical and motivational points to consider when approaching the subject of theme.

- Theme is not your characterization but the change of your characters, and the way they handle value systems reflects theme. Character arc reflects theme by showing how the various factors combine to obstruct and encourage your character in the accomplishment of a value-laden goal. This process most likely can result in a thematic impulse.

- Theme is the development of an idea that has meaning or significance. In a good story, the theme is not stated as a moral lesson but proved through the rigorous assignment of obstacles and victories for the protagonist. In other words, you never end a story with the "the moral of this story is . . . ." It must be proven through the action primarily of the Act Three climax. Ideas in literature have the ability to serve as motivation for teaching us how to live. It is oftentimes what your protagonist learns that makes him a better person by the time we reach the end. It holds together more tightly when it deals with life issues.

- Theme is not imagery, but imagery and image systems reflect, bolster, and sometimes even run against theme in the production.

- Theme is art equipping us for meaning. We want to have the idea of a piece proven to us visually. We crave meaning. We want to grow.

- Theme is unified. Your idea must be complete and self-contained within the fabric of the play. No footnotes allowed. No program notes to explain it. It should not be dependent on a discussion afterwards.

- Theme is about ethical values. Euripides's *Medea* (431 BC) is about the distinction between justice and revenge. Only when justice fails is one justified in claiming revenge. Medea is grossly mistreated by her husband. Does the killing of her own children to get back at her husband and his family justify this tragic act? In *Macbeth* (1606) the theme is the accumulation of deadly results that spring from greed for power. This is balanced by Macbeth's tremendous expressions of personal guilt.

- Theme is creating supporting characters who illustrate different aspects of the primary theme.

- Theme is not propaganda. Characters should not be mere mouthpieces for the author's message. The dialogue will descend to sloganeering or the recitation of editorials. Believe in something strongly, but present both sides of the argument.

It is interesting that playwrights are often reluctant to discuss what their play is about. Many are concerned that it will become a piece of propaganda, separating the theme from the action, isolating the idea which they know should be proven in the telling of the story. "Come see the show" or "Have you read the script?" are the prevalent responses.

Theme

## Discussion Questions and Exercises

1. Make a list of your concerns and preoccupations within today's culture and the state of our human condition that you might like to address in a play.

2. In terms of your theme, what vitally concerns you in terms of the human condition? Could your theme be considered in some manner to be equipping us, your audience, in how to live life? How is your own personal faith stance reflected in the nature of your theme?

3. Is your theme proven through the climactic actions of the Act Three climax?

# Chapter 14

# Dialogue, Monologue, and Subtext

CREATING EXCITING, PERTINENT, EFFICIENT, personality-reflective dialogue is at the heart of writing effective stories for the stage. The stage is dialogue dominant, especially when compared to most film, which is image dominant. Principles of writing dialogue that sings to the ear of your audience and is honest to the heart of your characters is a necessary artistic pursuit for the burgeoning playwright. It is interesting, but when I am directing a new play of either mine or another playwright, and an actor keeps stumbling over lines, or has trouble memorizing them, it is very often a problem with the truth factor in the dialogue. I immediately need to consider rewriting that line or lines as I continue the rehearsal process.

Who is your character? You must know the idiosyncrasies of your characters to write good dialogue. This extends to where they grew up, economic conditions, and cultural preferences—that is, their context. You must know the particulars. For example, a husband is telling his wife that he is leaving her and uses his dislike for broccoli, which she has just served him, as his "in" into the subject. He does not just come out and say, "I want a divorce." He is always hedging. He is always being oblique.

## Context

If you set up a *context*, i.e., action within an environment, then you are going to have richer dialogue and you are going to be able to approach the subject indirectly by talking about the activity. Always establish a context for a scene because it will shape your language, provide variety, differences in rhythm, builds, and volume levels. The scene below works itself out on this principle. Note how the context of one character sculpting a creative work grounds the sketch in a reality that is often referred to.

SKETCH: GOING ON . . . AND ON. . .

*(SHE has on a leather apron, goggles, and has a mallet and chisel miming working on a sculpture.)*

HE: *(enters)* Hey, Marge! Marge! *(SHE looks up.)* Looks ah . . . great.

SHE: Can't tell anything yet, I just started.

HE: Well, it certainly looks . . . solid.

SHE: Marble usually is.

HE: Marble—you don't mess around.

SHE: I want it to last.

HE: Like the pyramids, eh?

SHE: I want it to last longer than the pyramids. Would you stand over there please—flying chips.

HE: Sure. It looks . . . roundish.

SHE: Egg Shaped. Did you know the earth is essentially egg shaped? The womb is egg shaped. It's the universal form. Durable.

HE: You want it to fly?

SHE: I want it to be . . . resilient. I want it to go on long after I've gone. Would you hand me that thermos over there? You see, it's going to be an extension of me into the forever. "Dust to dust," "A blink of the eye," "but a fleeting moment in time," a "shrug of eternity"— bull! None of that for me. Look at this building? One good earthquake and it's a pile of rubble. Musical scores turn yellow and wither, tape loses its magnetic quality, dancers get bad knees, and celluloid? — why you're past tense as soon as the shutter clicks off. You ever notice how those old movie stars lock themselves up in their Beverly Hills mansions and play images of their youth repeatedly, dreaming about the past? Pathetic. You see this? This means that decades, even generations from now, I'll still be around.

HE: How will they know it's yours?

SHE: I'll put my initials on it. You know people talk about gaining immortality through their art. I'm more captivated, no consumed, by the idea of obtaining immortality by just . . . living forever. Now, do you mind?

   *(He sighs, exits as the chips fly.)*

As you can see, the dialogue is shaped by the activity of the artist which adds authenticity, variety, and interest.

## On the Nose Dialogue

*On the nose dialogue* is characterized by words and phrases that speak exactly what the character is feeling at the moment. You must save moments like this for climactic scenes, and, even then, use them sparingly. On the nose dialogue is used when people have explored all other strategies or opportunities to approach, persuade, or inform another character. For example, two characters talking about the sermon at church:

BOB: What did you think of the sermon, Amy? I know you have a thing against anything from the Old Testament. Well, this one was all about Noah and doing the right thing, and Noah's faith, and everybody else going to hell. I couldn't hear you snoring.

AMY: He didn't say anything I didn't know. God didn't even give the women names.

BOB: Yeah, tough times in the old Ark for the female libs. Like you.

AMY: I'm my own woman. I've found myself. But you, you could have learned something about obedience, even from the story of Noah, which is probably myth anyway. Like when the tide took your surfboard out when Dad told you not to. . .

BOB: Yeah, or like when Dad caught you and Schmidt in the backseat of the Buick.

AMY: Or like when . . . it was you who told him where I was. I hated you for that.

BOB: I know. Old news. And you didn't talk to me for a month.

AMY: Served you right.

BOB: Best of times.

AMY: I still feel I owe you one. You are the source of all my frustration.

## Breaking Up Dialogue

If you look at your page and all the speeches are the same length, go back and ask yourself if the characters are becoming your mouthpiece rather than their own mouthpiece. Conflict in dialogue builds like a tennis game: short shots, long shots, rushing for the net, high lobs, shots with spin on them which seem to go one way and then bounce another. Some technical ways of doing this are as follows:

- Have dialogue overlap occasionally.

- Do not finish all the sentences (though a reader will get very tired of ellipses [...] used without discretion.)

- A character's dialogue reflects their life rhythms. Find those rhythms and make sure they contrast with the other speaking characters.

- Do not get stuck in the question-answer trap. It is another expositional ploy.

- Dialogue should reflect the way someone thinks: some in a rush, others thoughtful and probing, still others as always challenging, verbose, always trying to make a joke, and the list goes on. If you truly understand the physical drive and idiosyncrasies of your character, then this will point toward a way of creating organic dialogue.

David Mamet, noted American playwright, provides a brief glimpse into the playful and broken nature of dialogue in *Glengarry, Glenn Ross* (1984):

MOSS: No. What do you mean? ...

AARONOW: Yes. I mean are you actually talking about this, or are we just ...

MOSS: No, we're just ...

AARONOW: We're just "talking" about it.

MOSS: We're just speaking about it. *[pause]* As an idea.

AARONOW: As an idea.

MOSS: Yes.

AARONOW: We're not actually talking about it.[1]

Note how the repetition provides flow and emphasis; note when the pauses are; note how the language is subtly about power. But the dialogue must always be driven by a purpose, so your dashes (—) and ellipses (. . .) might seem clever but if they do not serve character or action, they are just a writer's conceit.

## Do Not Be too Literary

A wry, cynical character with a PhD in English literature might be overly verbose; the same goes for a professional writer who is speaking to himself as much as to another, but most people do not speak poetry. T. S. Eliot's *The Cocktail Party* (1949), *Murder in the Cathedral* (1935), and Christopher Fry's *The Lady's Not for Burning* (1948) are all written in poetry. And because the authors are professional poets, these plays work. If you have equipped and educated yourself with the tools to produce a lyrical/literary side to your work, fine, go for it, but know that the commercial viability will work against it being produced. In writing a theatrical adaptation of Longfellow's poem, *The Courtship of Miles Standish* (2019), I found it a delightful but ongoing challenge to match his descriptive poetic powers while creating action and conflict to drive the dramatic through line.

William Shakespeare's work highlights both rhyming and unrhyming lyricism, but it is mostly in iambic pentameter, which is the natural speech structure of the English language. It should be noted that his lower-class comic characters either misspeak, digress, or are full of excess, and he uses them to temper the more tragic or intense dramatic moments in his plays.

So if you feature an erudite character, make sure he is balanced with a more earthy voice, like Eliza and Professor Higgins in George Bernard Shaw's *Pygmalion* (1913). Such erudite plays like *The Importance of Being Earnest* (1895) are carried by the wit and pacing of the language, though I find myself longing for a bit more of a cross section of humanity sounding off rather than the onslaught of mannered language which is not always as accessible as it might be. Even Sophocles brought a notable change in his elevated language with the introduction of the Herdsman and Messengers in *Oedipus Rex* (429 BC).

## Dialogue in Crisis and Climax

The crisis and climax are moments when dialogue is the most varied. Characters are under great stress. They say what they would never say under normal circumstances. This is where you can articulate the theme because the extreme tension of the action can carry it. This is where you can play against expected dialogue. This is the "moment of truth" for your central characters, so what they say is stripped of subterfuge and raw emotions and reactions emerge as plot situations become more revealing and demanding. Subtext usually goes out the window. So a man and woman spy are stuck in a room with a bevy of sharp shooters outside. They are leaning against a wall in between bursts of automatic fire. He says to her, "There's something I never told you . . ."

When you are writing within an established group—e.g., a bunch of undergrads, a football team locker room, teen girls at a pajama party—it is so easy to have all the characters sound the same so you must work extra hard to differentiate these characters. Even within a group of teen girls there is going to be some more grown up, others totally into gossip, some into make-up, someone in a crisis who must tell others about her problems, some with a secret, another with an annoying laugh, and so on.

"But that's how they really talked," might be true but it might not be appropriate to your story where you want to avoid stereotype while striving to provide unique individuality. Chit chat is not necessarily dialogue friendly because it can be so digressive. Certainly, characters can "change the conversation" but it is usually for a reason that the truth is being too closely approached and people are not ready for it. When you overhear dialogue in the workplace or at a coffee shop, listen for the repetition of words, for the inarticulate sounds that accompany dialogue, for the rhythm, for the tone, and for other phrases so you can capture and write them down and carry them with you. But when translating this to your characters' speech, be aware that now you are writing character and plot that is moving in a direction and that time cannot be wasted. And you are also creating words and sentences that are actor friendly.

Silences and pauses can have the same power as language. Isabella's silence in *Measure for Measure* (c. 1604) at the end when she finds she must marry the Duke, with no love being lost in their relationship, speaks volumes. Harold Pinter is a master at using the pause. Having directed several of Pinter's works, I have developed a great respect for where and why he uses pauses the way he does. They are always loaded with import. Pinter summed up his concept of silence in this quote of his, which can be considered his Pinter pause manifesto:

> I think that we communicate only too well, in our silence, in what's unsaid, and that what takes place is a continual evasion, desperate rearguard attempts to keep ourselves to ourselves. Communication is too alarming. To enter into someone else's life is too frightening. To disclose to others the poverty within us is too fearsome a possibility.[2]

Here is an excerpt from the opening to *Old Times* (1971) by Harold Pinter:

> Deeley, slumped in armchair, still.
>
> Kate curled on a sofa, still.
>
> Anna standing at the window, looking out.
>
> (Silence)
>
> Lights up on Deeley and Kate, smoking cigarettes.
>
> Anna's figure remains still in dim light at the window.
>
> KATE. [*reflectively*] Dark.
>
> > [*Pause*]
>
> DEELEY: Fat or thin?
>
> KATE: Fuller than me, I think.
>
> > (*Pause*)
>
> DEELEY: She was then?
>
> KATE: I think so.
>
> DEELEY: She may not be now.
>
> > (*Pause*)
>
> Was she your best friend?
>
> KATE: Oh, what does that mean?
>
> DEELEY: What?
>
> KATE: The word friend. . . when you look back. . . all that time.
>
> DEELEY: Can't you remember what you felt?

(*Pause*)

KATE: It is a very long time.[3]

They are talking about Anna, who is coming to visit Kate. Anna is representative of Kate's life before she met Deeley, and Kate is literally conjuring her up as she speaks. But as the drama reveals, Deeley is threatened by this prior relationship and is desperate to find out what his wife is up to and why.

## Subtext

In terms of dialogue, *subtext* has been likened to the tip of the iceberg. What has real relevance in the dialogue is underneath the water and what is implied, insinuated, hinted at, avoided, is above the water. As a writer you must know what is going on effectively in both places.

Why is learning to write subtext so important? Shakespeare, Jean Racine, the Greeks, and most classical drama, because of the literary density of the language, use subtext, or the hidden meaning of what is being said, less than contemporary writers. Perhaps this is because they were also so intent on communicating everything through the language itself and all its various literary forms.

Subtext is a process of misdirection, saying one thing but meaning another. It is an automatic tension-producing factor because the characters are trying to figure out what is going on while the audience is working to separate innuendo from truth as they begin to question the motives of characters. We, in real life, are constantly masking our true inner selves through covering up what we are really thinking or feeling. Not showing our weaknesses and vulnerabilities is the result of having spent a lifetime constructing verbal responses that cover up and spare us deeper introspection and discovery by other characters.

Dramatically, it is used to play two things at once, which every actor is looking for at every moment in the dialogue he is given by the playwright. So a soda jerk says to a pretty blonde, "you want a cherry on top?" and he is really saying, "I'm available, I'll give you anything you want." Or a church matron goes up to another sister in the Lord and says, "I'm praying for you, Anna, all the things you are going through. Tough things. I am here to help. Between us, me, and Him, good can come from all things bad. Right? Is there anything else I should be praying about?" What she is really looking for is to find out what Anna is going through so she can use it as a weapon.

It is a power play. Subtext is what agendas are made of. Subtext is the stuff of establishing personal strategies without other people knowing what you are doing. Subtext, more often than not, is about latent intent; it has an objective. It wants to seduce, or overpower, or discover, or relate without outwardly suggesting inward intent.

## Language as Action

Physical action and language are interrelated—one demands the other. You squirm when you do not want to say something and use a lot of "uhs" and "well's"; you use language to run away from someone, to make someone cower, to shame someone, to make them shake with fear or laugh. In other words, language as dialogue becomes a weapon. If you think of language as having a physical effect on another person, then you will be looking for language as action. What you are really doing is finding the conflict base of good dialogue.

Interestingly, *onomatopoeia*—i.e., the formation of a word from a sound associated with what is named—works along these lines. So, words like bombast, drudge, whip, blunt, drizzle, hallelujah, and swoon are all words that sound like the actions they represent. An actor will shape her dialogue and physical actions around such words as these, giving them a shape verbally, and perhaps even physically through gesture. All of this empowers the use of language. Are you conscious of the evocative power of language used to create a visceral and sensory response rather than just an intellectual understanding?

## Strategies

Dialogue is directly connected to a character's objectives. A good scene does not allow the character to achieve his objectives in an easy manner. Sometimes she does not achieve them at all. Ask yourself what strategies she might use and how this might affect your dialogue? For example, your character berates his daughter for getting pregnant. He says it is not his business, so he pleads with her to understand his situation. He is always thinking about himself, but then breaks down and cries to let her know how broken he is. He then ridicules her for being weak and sniveling. The dialogue and changing strategies in this scene reveal character as well as actions.

In summary, as it pertains to writing dialogue:

- Dialogue must always show character.
- Repetition can be used for building emphasis, or it can be boring.
- Do not be afraid to have a character be a liar.
- Write lines that demand a response.
- Always talk from an angle, from a personal perspective, a point of view.
- Let dialogue be shaped to the class, ethnicity, environment, education, and age of your characters.
- Always be aware in each scene of what the character wants and what is stopping the character from getting whatever it is.
- Know your character's backstory and when to bring it into play. Write specifics and write details.
- Do not take sides. Honestly explore the objectives of both characters in conflict.
- When your characters speak, it is usually to get something.
- Read it out loud. Have others read it out loud.

Look at Jesus in terms of the way that he used language. He asked a lot of questions, and often addressed a question with a question in return. He told stories and sometimes explained their meaning and sometimes did not. He liked to use imagery. He was direct in accusing people of their hypocrisy, and he refused to address the leaders of the Sanhedrin and Pontius Pilate directly. In his language he referred to the things around him that he saw: plants, walls, gates, water, trees, sheep, and so forth.

## Writing a Monologue and Soliloquy

A *monologue* is technically a somewhat long speech by one person which is usually addressed to another person or persons in the immediate vicinity. It is usually story oriented, depending on the process of memory. The other person can be referred to, even reacted to, when the actor/character is performing her monologue.

A *soliloquy*, on the other hand, is the character voicing her inner thoughts or telling a story without the cognizance of someone else being present. It can be *inner driven*, in which the audience is not acknowledged, or *outer driven*, where the audience is directly addressed. I have seen productions of *Hamlet* (c. 1600) in which the "To be or not to be" speech is played as an intensely personal inner-driven speech and, in another case, as a highly sardonic interpretation in which the Dane consciously addresses the audience during his delivery. I have even seen it delivered as a monologue, in which Hamlet speaks to the sleeping Ophelia. In short, the soliloquy is essentially a long speech that speaks inner thoughts or tells a story, has a beginning, middle, and end, and is delivered by a single actor/character to himself or to the audience as audience.

The monologue offers insights into the emotional and mental workings of the character's psyche. It is natural if you are performing a scene with another actor to resort to subtext and to not reveal all the truth because of the natural defenses that we put up in a social situation. One of the advantages of the monologue is that these defenses can come down a bit as the character shares his inner most thoughts and desires. When a character launches into a longer speech it is because something has happened in which they have to tell this story, or this bit of information, *now*. So there is often an emotional component to it.

The person doing the monologue is talking to someone else. They are in the same space. It is not a voice-over as someone reads a letter, or a soliloquy (which Shakespeare's *Hamlet* does so much of). For example, a father is telling his son how he played college baseball and tried to make it to the big leagues and what happened that prevented this, to assure his son that we set goals, but we do not always make them, and it is okay.

A monologue usually takes the form of a story rather than just a lot of emotional outpouring. It looks back, or forward. But remember, it is not just reminiscing, it is a story that your teller needs to tell someone else, now!

A good monologue has a natural build leading to a climax. This does not mean that you are yelling at someone, or breaking down, it just means that as you get to the reason why you are telling the story there is a commitment in desire and energy to get the message through.

The language of a monologue can be a bit more lyrical than just conversational. It is not as limited as the language of dialogue. It can also include the speaker becoming another character as a technique. For example, "So he says to me, in that west Texas drawl of his, 'Bobby, you ain't seen anything 'till you seen me kill weeds by pissin' on 'em.'"

Your story should have internal tension within the teller (how hard is it to tell this story?) and within the story itself. It should not be just anecdotal. It must count. It must reveal. Ask yourself what the obstacles are that the teller has to go through to tell this story.

The following are examples of monologues.

**Example no. 1**: From *Paper Wings* (1995). Stan is sub-textually expressing his frustration with Jamie becoming a believer and he, like the pigs, being an outsider:

> *(STAN is standing in front of television, JAMIE is curled up in sofa facing him. He has Bible open. Snaps it shut and throws it down. Picks up drink.)*

STAN: Now I ask you - what about the pigs? A bright, blue-sky day in the region of the Gadarenes. Pigs rooting about - who said the Jews never ate pork? An innocent day, pig snout, pig snort, rough bristling hair rubbing up, pig skin, pig smell. Just like any other day. In the pig pen. Down on the farm. Mort rooting with the rest, tubers, greens, sow scent. "Ummm! Eat now. Then a good roll in the mud. Noise! Keep chewing. Noise nearer now. Man-thing. yelling, jump, Mort keep an eye out. Man throws stones, man beat with sticks." The herd stirs, heads lift, mouths grind as the naked man runs, circling, making swine noises.

> *(STAN makes some of these noises.)*

"Circle the wallow, throwing stones, beating pig flesh with thorny switch. Pain sound. Blood smell stirs. Mort watch out." Then he comes, another man, grace, graceful and touches the madness. Voices come out, spitting, snarling, growling, whining. Legions launched, let go - where? On the pigs, in the pigs. Why the pigs? "Pigs run. Mort run. Red eye, crazed eye — pigs not pigs. Mort caught in crush of pig hair. Mort try to stop. No! No! Water smell. Hooves dig in. Others push. Over cliff. Pig squeal in the rush-go-by."

Mort was non-possessed you see, one of the few demon free who in the very push of madness was carried along, an innocent bystander, a piece of green still stuck in the flap-corner of his mouth. And dim thoughts of seagull wings came to his pig brain.

"Wings flap, flap then fly. Mort fly."

And he flapped his pig legs like this, like this . . . with all the concentration and fury that he possessed among hurtling bodies and the stink of pig fear. "Then 'slap' water hit, breath blown out, pink flesh pushes down, down, snout point up, up . . . Legs work up down, up down to fly. Darkness."

And then pig bloat, and swollen bodies bob in the gentle waves of the Sea of Galilee near the region of the Gadarenes.

(*Pause.*)

So, what about the bloody pigs?

(*Lights.*)[4]

**Example no. 2**: The following is from my play *Five Cups of Coffee* (2006), which deals with Frank's working class truck driver's background and presents the source of so much of his personal anger:

FRANK FUSCHIANO: My old man? His name was Antonio Fuschiano. You want to know how he died? I'll tell you. It was a work accident. At least that's what they called it. He was causin' trouble with the Company, talkin' strike. They found him stuck down in the hold of one of those oil cargo ships up to here in the tar sediment. He musta yelled all night. They found him standing up over his knees in muck, deader than a doornail. The fumes . . . but it wasn't no "accident." They left him down there. So, it was Standard Oil that killed my father. The family split up. I joined the Union in order to make 'em pay. The Union —that became my family. A trucker. I delivered Standard Oil gasoline. And every time I opened the gas locks in the stations—I'd spit in them.

(*He spits.*)

That's for Papa. That's for Mama. That's for the Old Country that spit us up on these shores in Newark, New Jersey after the war and forgot about us. Families are all screwed up these days. The Union, they took care of you. Only trouble now is that they don't do nothin' anymore. Used to have a reputation for rabble-rousin,' goin' on strike. Now all's they do is send a letter upstairs askin' for more dainty wipes in the guy's John. That's why I quit truckin.' Drove from Newark to Seattle and stepped down and never climbed up into the big rigs again. Almost thirty years later and I still can't get the stink of gasoline from under my nails. Thirty years, now that's real time. You, yeah you fruit head. You wanna know what time is? Time is a punch card stained with the grease on your hands. No grease, you haven't done your time. But the best time? — quittin' time. That's the best time of all.[5]

## Discussion Questions and Exercises

1. Context. Writing dialogue in context means writing speech within the context of an on-going action. This cannot help but to enliven the nature of the dialogue. Select a context moment in your script and write it out, making sure the activity plays an organic and meaningful part in the conflict in the scene. Or write an original scene using a context you are familiar with as two characters relate to each other.

2. Subtext. Subtext is language which implies meaning. In other words, like a huge iceberg, the part that is showing is the tip (the dialogue) but the "real" meaning is submerged. So in this scene people talk around what they are feeling but be sure to keep the conversation going on either the mattress or the wedding dress.

   • A mattress store: a senior couple is going to buy what will probably be their last mattress; or a middle-aged couple near separation are buying a mattress, the wife's last-ditch effort to hold things together; or two teenagers are thinking of moving in and living together but they are not married. Create a scene in which they talk about their feelings through the way they relate to the mattress. You can add a third character of a salesman if you want. OR

   • An attic: in which a middle-aged couple is rummaging around in the attic and the wife or husband discover the original wedding dress. Describe what is going on between them primarily by writing about the wedding dress. OR

   • Take two of your characters from your story idea. Put them in a tense situation that explores emotions and conflict and write a subtextual scene that might happen between them. It does not need to be an actual scene from your script.

# Chapter 15

# Some Thoughts on Getting Started

IT MAY SEEM A DAUNTING TASK to get a play written, re-written, read, cast, and ultimately performed. A novelist must find a single publishing company and perhaps an agent in his process. Producing plays, symphonies, and film scripts have the difficulty of creation and the difficulty of assembling a significant cast of people both on the stage and backstage to make them happen artistically. The good news is that you can do it cheaper and a lot quicker than the larger media venues. The excitement about the theater is that you can make it happen. It will not cost you millions of dollars. What it does take is a love for theater, a belief in your product, and the persistence to see it through until it is "curtain up."

This chapter is not a compendium on all the professional venues, play contests, faith-based, or theater companies. Neither is it about how to secure copyright, whether you should join the Dramatist's Guild, or how to get an agent. Rather I am going to write anecdotally about my journey as a writer and what areas of success and failure I have had over the years in getting my work performed.

## Getting Started

In the early sixties, I was a pre-med English major at Tulane University. My senior year, last semester, I took a playwriting class, and my one-act was selected, along with a few others, to be featured in a no budget production on campus. I got the theatrical bug. Medicine be hanged. I applied for graduate school in the playwriting program, somehow got accepted, and was launched into writing plays. I soon discovered, however, that I knew nothing about how plays worked or how they were put up, so I changed my emphasis and went into acting and directing, hoping that in these disciplines something would rub off to make me a better writer. It is a process I highly recommend. Knowing what the actor and director go through to launch your work or any play on the live stage is an essential ingredient to knowing how to write a play. I then spent a bit of time in Vietnam and left to become the director of a small university theater department in Lexington, Kentucky. No writing. But reading a lot of plays, directing several plays, and teaching theater history, acting, and directing laid a groundwork that would pay off later as I began to write.

A few years later, after joining the University of Pittsburgh theater department, getting my PhD from Florida State University, and spending almost a year in England researching the relationship between writers and a professional theater in the Midlands, I became a Christian. I was around thirty years old and was well versed in the acting and directing aspects of theater but was still peripherally into the writing area. After just a few months as a new convert, I was searching for some sort of venue for realizing my theatrical talents in a faith-based manner. That is when I met the Reverend Roger Green, who was head of an organization called Children's Sand and Surf Mission (CSSM), an offshoot of Scripture Union. CSSM did outreach programs for kids on the beaches during the summer. They recruited a group of college students and adults and mounted a two-week beach experience with stories, puppets, songs, Bible study, swimming, games, and a host of other Bible-based activities presented every weekday morning. They did this up and down the eastern seaboard. My wife BJ and I and our two boys headed for Myrtle Beach, South Carolina, where I was told by Roger to start writing sketches for kids, one a day, ten sketches in two weeks. Right!? I had not been a believer long enough to even read the Old Testament, so when he told me I had to write a sketch about Abraham and Sarah I asked with some trepidation, "Abraham who?" While the rest of the team swam and relaxed in the afternoons, I prayed with great humility and created sketches about Abraham, Daniel, a few parables, Jonah, Noah, and a smattering more. What a great way for me to learn Scripture. Each sketch lasted about ten minutes, and I had to depend totally on the inspiration and guidance of the Holy Spirit. We rehearsed the sketch in the late afternoon, the next morning before breakfast, and performed "off book" on the beach for up to 120 kids a couple of hours later—every day.

What I learned from this experience was how to take narrative material and theatricalize it, how to add humor, write songs that could be easily learned, and how to involve our young audiences in a participatory format. The players were untrained, and I so enjoyed watching them form a cohesive group and gain confidence performing for children. I started with the easiest age group to write for (ages 5–12), and it bolstered my confidence and sense of usefulness as a writer. No pay. Just the joy of dramatic play for children on one of God's beautiful playgrounds. I also gained a love for writing for children and signed up to teach a children's theater class at the University of Pittsburgh. I was able to stage lengthier and more challenging works out of this class by touring productions to the Pittsburgh greater geographical area. Ultimately, we paid student actors and I saw my plays produced in schools and other venues by the Childsplay Theater Company that was created out of the class.

You see how one thing leads to another? I believe that is how God develops us and our talents to serve him. Start simple. Learn your craft. Writing for church and missions can result in writing for long term professional arenas and open greater ministry possibilities. After over twenty years working for CSSM, I had more than 100 sketches for kids that were being disseminated to all the beach mission groups which had now expanded to the gulf and west coasts as well as the inner city, Children's Street and Sidewalk Missions. Two books of my Bible-oriented sketches have been published by Lillenas Press and now by Wipf and Stock. Appendix 1 is a lengthy essay with examples on how to write the theatrical sketch.

> *"For whoever has despised the day of small things shall rejoice. . ."*
>
> —Zech. 4:10 (NRSV)

I had written a small musical two-hander titled *Abraham and Sarah* (1981) as a family-based drama but had no producing resource in Pittsburgh that could put it on. So I decided to produce it myself, acting the part of Abraham, casting a musically talented Sarah (Ginger Auld), getting a composer/musician as the accompanist (Rick Conrad), finding a church basement with a credible stage area, and mounting the show directed by Kate McConnell. We served soup and bread and then performed. By the end of the run, we had full houses and realized there was an audience out there for our work. The lesson here? Do not always wait around for somebody else to do your plays, especially when starting out as a writer. Find a way to do them yourself. Make them happen. *Abraham and Sarah* was subsequently picked up by several professional companies and received numerous productions throughout the U.S., Canada, and Central America.

Out of this beginning experiment, a professional company was birthed called Saltworks Theater Company, which is still in existence today, over thirty years later. It is staffed with faith-based administrators, directors, and actors, providing a living wage for all participants. The theater company's original impetus came from a continuing grant from St. Francis Hospital, who provided $100,000 for the company to tour social-action dramas dealing with such subjects including drug addiction and treatment for youth, AIDS prevention, teenage sexuality, good touch-bad touch, and bullying. As one of the founders of this theater company, I was also privileged over the years to do most of the writing for the forty-five-minute dramas that toured to elementary, middle, and high school audiences. I have also created one-hour, small-cast, six-actor adaptations of Shakespeare which have been widely performed and published, for example, *Shakespeare-On-The-Go* (2015).

Writing for children on the beaches bore fruit in writing for children at the University of Pittsburgh, writing for children and youth for Saltworks Theater, writing Shakespeare adaptations for children for the professional Three Rivers Shakespeare Company, and creating feature length children's shows that are performed by faith-based and secular theater companies around the country. The social action dramas I created for Saltworks Theater were picked up by numerous regional professional companies as part of their own educational touring operations. The lesson here? As a writer, wear as many hats as you can. I was now wearing the children's ministry hat, the social action theater hat, the educational theater hat, and the professional theater hat. I was also creating dramas that had a redemptive function and that, being of a touring nature, had a long and extensive royalty life.

I also recommend that wherever you are living, thoroughly investigate the possibilities of writing for and about the community. For Pittsburgh I created, with Attilio Favorini, *Steel/City* (1976), a staged musical documentary about the historical, cultural, and economic impact of the industry on the city. It also toured to the mill towns on the rivers in the area on a performance barge and was featured at the Smithsonian Folk Festival in 1976. Out of this was born a professional company that produced Shakespeare every year. What are your local schools' curricula teaching? Could you write plays on these works, on the history of the city, on writers and poets and artists and dancers of note that came from your town? In other words, find the need and fill it.

For my PhD research, I worked under the head of the BBC Radio Drama, Martin Esslin, a noted critic and author. I was fascinated with the work being done at the Victoria Theater in Stoke-on-Trent, a professional theater in the round that had started the musical documentary movement in England. They created shows on the Pottery Industry (Spode and Wedgewood China come from there), the local train and steel industries, and on the founder of Primitive Methodism, William Clowes. One of these, *Hands Up for You the War is Ended* (1971), deals with Stoke prisoners of war during World War 2, their escape adventures in Italy, and the stories of their wives surviving at home. The famed Victorian novelist Arnold Bennett came from Stoke and the theater staged several adaptations of his full-length works as well as his short stories. As a cultural institution, the theater became as important to the life of this gritty Midlands town as the baker and the butcher. The lesson here? Do not write a dissertation on some esoteric subject that will not challenge and feature your future creative and academic pursuits. And fully investigate the historical and cultural potentiality of your domain.

Leaving Pittsburgh and going to Regent University in Virginia Beach, Virginia, to teach in their graduate theater and film programs afforded me additional opportunities to write and produce my own theatrical fare. While in full-time residency there, I wrote numerous full-length plays and musicals on biblical personalities and contemporary dramas that deal with faith issues. Many of these works have found further production opportunities in a host of Christian-based universities nationally and professional companies. Getting a university to produce your work is a way to be recognized by other universities as well as by professional venues that are always looking for new, relevant, and exciting plays. The performance run-time is limited, but worth getting involved.

Other faith-based activities on my writing journey have taken me to The Lamb's Players during the 1980s in Times Square, for The Man Called Jesus, a Virginia Beach based company, which has toured a cut-down biblical narrative play to several foreign countries, and a full-scale musical produced by the Willow Creek Church. While in Pittsburgh I wrote and directed several parables for The Parable Players out of Ascension Episcopal Church. The play toured successfully for about eight years, used about twenty different actors, including paid actors and church members for each performance.

Another important venue to consider is the one-person play. Find an exceptionally talented actor and write a piece that would prove popular to a wide-ranging audience. A good friend of mine, Roger Nelson, toured a one-person show on Wesley written by Brad L. Smith, *The Man from Aldersgate* (1984), for several decades. Consider the mileage he got out of this over that time, taking it throughout the world. I have written a handful of one person shows for Carol Jaudes, who was in *Cats* (1981) on Broadway for several years, and who is involved with regional arts direction for the Salvation Army. I have adapted several of my biblically oriented dramas to a one-person format to provide venues for graduating MFA student actors as they go out into the professional world.

Having taught at a Christian University for almost thirty years, I had the opportunity to see many very talented theater students after graduation start their own theater companies. Many of them have produced my plays, so keeping in touch and networking is a must for the playwright looking for productive dissemination of his work. This is important, because there are very few agents working exclusively for faith-based writers, and most of the secular-based agents are not interested.

In getting started in your local area, the idea is to create a track record so that you can establish your input as a writer into a variety of creative, historical, educational, and industrial areas. For example, I was hired by Alcoa Aluminum to put up a weekly mounting of short sketches dealing with working problems and interpersonal relationships on the job in the foyer of the headquarters building in Pittsburgh. This came about because of the success of *Steel/City* as both an educational theater and professional theater endeavor. Another time I created a show called *Who Cares* (1988) which toured to medical schools, churches, and Senior Care Centers and which dealt with alcohol problems with the elderly. It was participatory and encouraged audience interaction. Its origin could be traced to the social action theater work I had already established in the local area. As you investigate your locale look for the needs that it is experiencing and ask yourself how your writing inclinations and your love for theater art could meet these needs.

Some concrete suggestions would begin with investigating the writing possibilities in your area. Start with your church. Approach your pastor with some ideas about sermon teasers or even more effective, get a handful of actors together to do sketches for the elementary aged kids in the church school. Write for church seasonal celebrations. I think I have written at least twelve short theater sketches dealing with Good Friday. It became a tradition at our church.

Contact your local schools and find out what the curriculum in the reading areas are for elementary, middle, and high schools in your area. If they are reading the book *Diary of a Wimpy Kid* (2007), find out if you can get the theatrical rights and go to work. Or create a children's version called

"Young Pilgrim's Progress" with no royalty restrictions. Almost all high schools offer some exposure to Shakespeare. Can you create a small cast version of *Macbeth* (1606) or *Comedy of Errors* (c. 1594)? I also wrote a play titled *Circus Machine* (1982) which literally took over an elementary school in McKeesport, Pennsylvania for three days with workshops in acting and mime work, photography, mural painting, and rhythmic dance improvisation. At the end of these sessions the play was performed and the children who had participated found themselves in the drama as well as seeing their artwork realized as a backdrop for the show itself.

Find out if there are any poets or novelists or historical persons of note in your area whose story creation might offer up lively theatrical production material and propose it to schools and to local producing entities. Is there a local industry that you could create a historical show about? Perhaps in your area there is a lumber industry, or a paper-making industry, or something of similar importance. Write about its background, interview former workers, find out what is in the future, and craft dramatic scenes and even musical numbers to make it super entertaining. There are real funding possibilities here.

In addition, you can start a writing group. It could begin as a reading group. Set a goal of putting on scenes from your efforts which could be put up in various venues, starting with someone's living room.

And if you have acting ability, write a one-person show for yourself, or for someone with acting talent. This is a tremendously flexible venue since a one-person show can be put up just about any place. I have written a couple of plays that feature a sequence of monologues, mostly on Bible-based characters and famous Christian historical figures which can be done by a single actor or by many. If you are just starting out, the important thing is to keep reading plays, going to plays, acting in shows, and enacting your characters. And do not write plays with huge numbers of characters and expansive set requirements.

The possibilities are limited by one's imagination and available time. At the onset these will hardly provide a living wage and will be essentially avocational in nature. But I have found that avocations are the stepping-stones to professional possibilities.

In summary, wear as many writer-friendly hats as you can to include the educational, ministry, social action, and professional theater venues. Do not be shy about writing without a guarantee of getting paid because building a network and getting produced are just as important as getting paid when you first start out. Aggressively pursue all kinds of theater contacts, look for publication possibilities, and enter playwriting contests. Christians in Theater Arts (CITA) has a yearly playwriting contest which I highly recommend one consider entering. Hone your skills as a film and television writer, read plays as if it was going out of style, and go to the theater whenever you can. Network with theater organizations and join or start a faith-based writing group that has credible membership. Finally, and most important, pray to our Father for wisdom, perseverance, and creative callings. Ask him to anoint and bless your imagination.

Good writing.

## Discussion Questions and Exercises

1. Create a theatrical demographic of your geographical location. Where are the theaters? Who is touring to the schools, find out what you can about them, including fees, transportation, and the subject matter that schools are buying and that have been particularly successful in the past? What are the important historical characters and literary figures that have come from your area? Investigate their work and think in terms of adapting their contributions to the stage. What about the museums in your area? Do you think they would like to see actors performing the life of a painting and the artist who created it as groups came through? What are the local organizations that support artists and artistic creation? How could you convince a shoe company that they could use your services and how it would help the bottom line as well as enhance their community visibility?

2. Contact your church first, and then others. Can you sell them on the idea of doing a presentation in your church? During the COVID-19 lockdown, our church went on YouTube and we created a duo playing Frank and Emma, married seniors, who confronted all sorts of problems. It could then be transposed live to services once things opened up. Your church also has a denominational history that most likely contains more than enough dramatic material to keep you researching and writing everything from sketches to full-length dramas that could also go national in terms of spreading through your denomination.

# APPENDICES

# Appendix 1

## Writing the Sketch

What's the "sketch"?

Traditionally the sketch is a short (6–10) minute dramatic representation that can be used in several different venues:

- Sermon teasers
- School programs
- Retreats
- Street theater
- Ice breakers

Hopefully, they will be created so they can be put together with a couple of one-hour rehearsals using a small cast, no major set requirements, no special effects, a minimum of props and featuring a single dramatic theme that can be produced on just about any stage or found space.

Sketches are designed to provide, awaken, and reflect on a certain thematic preoccupation such as tithing or the tongue, faith and folly, and matters dealing with less esoteric issues like Christian living and discipline. They are not meant to sum up all the tenants of the faith in eight short minutes, or to offer definitive answers to complex or even paradoxical theological questions. They should offer an insight, a question, a bit of character, some humor and be structured so that they have a beginning, a middle, and an end. Above all, they should be entertaining.

The Bible itself, from a narrative standpoint, offers a sweeping overview of God's evolving plan for mankind from Creation to the Second Coming. The sketch, or any dramatic presentation for that matter, can reflect just a moment in this great panoply of divine revelation. And being drama, it is more often concerned with a character reaction, an emotional epiphany, or a dramatic action that puts the wider vision of Scripture into an immediate and accessible perspective. In other words, it personalizes Scripture through dialogue and action and allows us to identify with what is happening in a way that the Bible itself does not always get around to doing. Thus, a sketch might explore the emotional context of a character, putting him in a context that we can identify with. When we see Martha fretting in the kitchen (context) as she is experiencing anger and impatience (emotion) with her sister Mary, who is having trouble focusing on her housekeeping responsibilities because of her adoration over the visiting Jesus in the next room, we identify with both women in an immediate way.

**Uses of the Sketch: Sermon Teaser**. One of the most popular uses of the sketch is to present a dramatic scene during the service which will complement, highlight, or set up the primary questions of the sermon delivered later by the minister. Thus, a drama depicting the deleterious effects of water cooler gossip in the workplace undergirds and serves as a reference point for the minister's sermon on "the tongue" in the Letter of James.

During a service at Wells Cathedral in Somerset, England, David Watson, accompanied by a team from the Riding Lights Theater Company and a small dance ensemble from his church, would stop his sermon for short periods of time while the artists performed dramatic and kinesthetic interludes that either reflected points of interest that he had already made in the sermon or illustrated references yet to be articulated.

The sketches should not simply retell the story in Scripture but should provide a certain "take" on the subject at hand. It is important, also, that the sketch is not preachy or a sermon in itself, but through character and action provide a metaphor for the truth being expounded from Scripture.

**Preaching Reference**. Ministers can utilize the drama-oriented material to amplify and spice up the material that they are delivering in a sermon. This can be accomplished by quoting examples from the plays or playing one of the characters (especially in the monologues) for dramatic effect. Variety, humor, and a different point of view are the desired results providing another way of grounding the biblical story through dramatic effects using the first person. For example, the minister could become the character of David as he replays his guilt feelings with Bathsheba, or he assumes the character of the father who is trying to convince his daughter not to be unequally yoked to a non-believer in an impending marriage situation. How often have we found that the moments which most provoke us in a sermon, and which stay with us afterwards are those preceded by the minister's "Let me tell you a story. . ." or "imagine that we were walking down that road to Emmaus" or "this reminds me of a man I knew who. . ."

**Ice Breaker**. Any dramatic event is going to excite more than just the cognitive areas of the brain but will also stimulate the associational—"that sounds just like my father," the emotional, "I felt the same way when I was going forward to be prayed for," and the contextual, "he thinks his office environment is a breeding ground for temptation, he ought to see mine!" Within this identification complex the audience who views these sketches/monologues will have a field of reference points that will often be much broader than the three points made by a well-structured sermon or teaching session. As such, the audience will be more willing to participate and share personal reactions on both a cognitive and emotional level. So perform your sketches at youth rallies, Lenten series, for special church calendar events, school assemblies, conferences, and such. They cannot take the place of a lengthy talk or sermon from the standpoint of content, but they can invigorate the atmosphere to encourage more active participation from the audience.

## How to Stage the Sketch

Every producing organization is going to have different requisites to consider when staging the dramatic sketch. Considerations of personnel, time, space and rehearsal restraints, and financial support will vary from church to church and school to school. Other books have dealt with great specificity on how to mount a production under less than favorable situations, so I will briefly sum up what I consider to be the "musts" when contemplating starting a drama ministry in your church or a drama program in your school, camp, or institution that is focused on presenting the sketch.

- You **must** have a person who can lead the troupe and who knows how to conduct rehearsals, to block the shows, to motivate actors, and to serve as the visionary force behind the drama program or troupe. This is usually the Director. It is extremely difficult to even contemplate starting a drama ministry without the leadership of someone who is trained in theater production techniques. Without this person there will be the possibility for contentiousness during rehearsals, for arguments over leadership, and for the flagrant waste of everyone's valuable time.

- You **must** have a minimum of three rehearsals, each of a couple of hours in length, to ensure that the actors have time to identify with the character and memorize the lines. You should also rehearse on the same day that you perform.

- You **must** ensure that your production can be seen and heard by the audience. Nothing is more frustrating than a sketch that is played with one character sitting on his knees and the congregation cannot see the actor because there is little or no rake where the audience is seated. These shows are usually with a small cast so go ahead and use lavaliere mics whenever possible, making sure that you have a competent person on the sound equipment and making sure that mics are charged and tested before the performance.

- You **must** think of using appropriate props when mounting these sketches. Since there are few elaborate costumes or set pieces that are normally constructed for an eight-minute sketch, the use of a strategic prop can truly help to create a dramatic moment between actors. So do not mime the fruit in the Adam and Eve scene; Gomer needs her suitcase, it speaks of her comings and goings; and the young man on his first date is defined by the little notebook that he carries. If the sketch or monologue does not call for a prop, think about including one anyway. Props make the context, or environment, of the scene happen, and they are another vehicle through which character relationship can be realized.

- You **must** be cognizant of energy and pacing in your sketch. Pure energy can make up for a lack of expertise in actor training. This does not mean that you rush through your lines, or inordinately force the tempo of the scene, it just means that you are conscious of having actors enter and exit in a timely fashion. While actors are onstage they must really want something—in acting terms this is called their objective or goal. Also be sure that they are actively concentrating on what is going on during the stage action, and that they are committed to the moment, to what is happening in the context of the scene. Look for the climax of the sketch. It is here where the payoff is. It is just such a plot point moment that should be played with excitement and anticipation and perhaps desperation.

- You **must** differentiate between the characters. Look for those traits in your character that define them: the down to earth, no nonsense character of Thomas; Angelica, the business woman, is always on the go, always in a whirl; and Solomon, though a politician on the outside, on the inside reveals that he is defensive and even feeling somewhat guilty.

Some examples of sketch writing can be found in the following:

### Sketch: The Words We Say

James 3–8 (NIV): "But no one can tame the tongue; it is a restless evil and full of deadly poison."

*(An office atmosphere. At the cooler.)*

SHE: I saw three of them coming out this morning.

HE: Of the conference room?

SHE: Yes. Aren't you going to ask me who it was?

HE: Gladys? And Rich.

SHE: That's right. And . . . Martin Ewbank.

HE: The quiet types always surprise you.

SHE: He was fixing his tie.

HE: Are you sure?

*(SHE nods.)*

SHE: First it was just Gladys and Rich.

HE: And now they've added. . . Martin.

SHE: You know Priscilla, well she's always the first one here. She says that they're always here on Tuesdays before she is.

HE: That's early. With the door closed I suppose . . .

SHE: That's right.

HE: Sounds to me like a . . .

SHE: *Ménage à trois*—exactly what I was thinking. Of course, we could be wrong.

HE: Of course.

SHE: Poor Marge.

HE: You mean Marge, Rich's wife?

SHE: Mmmmm. And Gladys being a divorcee . . .

HE: Where does Martin fit in?

SHE: I'd rather not know.

(They laugh.)

SHE: I've said little things, dropped little hints.

HE: The wife is always the last to know.

SHE: Like "How are things with Rich?" and "You two getting along alright?"

HE: Nothing overt.

SHE: Heavens no.

HE: I mean, when you get right down to it, it's really not our business is it?

SHE: You're right, this is the new millennium.

HE: Live and let live. I'm O.K., you're O.K.

SHE: We had a 9 a.m. budget meeting in there this morning. When I walked in I said, "Whew, this place smells like the men's locker room," and I opened the window.

HE: In front of Snyder?

SHE: I said it as sort of a joke. Had them all sniffing. Of course Bartlby came out with the expected . . .

HE: "How do you know what the men's locker room smells like, Janice?" And Snyder?

SHE: He was only into budgets . . .

HE: You know, I heard that his daughter . . .

SHE: Everyone's heard that.

HE: So, what are you going to do?

SHE: About . . . ?

HE: Gladys.

SHE: I'm having lunch with Gladys.

HE: You're going to ask her?

SHE: There are ways of finding out without asking.

HE: You'll let me know?

SHE: Water cooler at 2.

HE: It's a date.

SHE: Shhh! I'm a married woman. We don't want to start any rumors now do we?

> *(Three hours later, indicated by having both actors turn, then come back. Both arrive with water cooler cups.)*

HE: Well?

SHE: We had a nice chat. I had fish. She had fettuccini with clam sauce.

HE: With clams – wouldn't you guess.

SHE: I got around to talking about Herb Gladstone leaving his family and running off with the little 'ethnic' tart from the typing pool and I sort of mentioned: "You know Gladys, people are beginning to say things about you and Rich—early morning things."

HE: You came right out and said it?

SHE: Well, let me tell you, she got all flustered, couldn't eat her pasta. I've never seen her like that.

HE: The mousetrap.

SHE: The what?

HE: You know, in Hamlet, when . . .

SHE: Yes, yes. Finally she composed herself and without batting an eyelash said she was meeting with Rich and now Martin every Tuesday morning for a . . . get this . . . a Bible study.

HE: She said that?

SHE: She said that some very interesting things were happening in her life.

HE: I'll bet.

SHE: And that she'd found God or something like that . . . you know, something that sounded like one of those bumper stickers.

HE: She said that? Gladys? You didn't believe her, did you?

SHE: Not for a second. Especially when she asked me if I'd like to come.

HE: Quartet! Now wait a minute, you didn't say yes, did you?

SHE: I was tempted—she was all sort of secret and glowing—I would have loved to call her bluff, but I begged off saying that it was hard enough for me to get to work by nine what with the kids and husband. I really hit "kids" and "husband"—you know.

HE: Wait until I tell Ralph. This is hotter than the latest installment of "Love for Life."

SHE: Cheers.

*(They laugh and toast their water cups. SHE speaks facetiously.)*

Here's to "The Good News." Oh, by the way, how are you and Sheila doing?

HE: Fine. Great.

*(Pause. SHE exits.)*

Why?

SHE: Terrific. You know it would really surprise me if something went wrong with your marriage. See ya.

*(Pause.)*

HE: Yeah!

*(Slowly crumples up his cup. End.)*

## SKETCH: TIMES HAVE CHANGED

Ruth 4:6 (Amplified Bible): "Take my right of redemption yourself, for I cannot redeem it."

> *(Two chic looking women are holding champagne glasses as they look at paintings on the wall.)*

MARGE: It's the latest thing. Made from kitchen products—napkins, paper towels, saran wrap, aluminum, baggies, you name it.

LIZ: So, what does it say?

MARGE: You're not supposed to ask that. You don't ask "what does it mean" or "what is it." It's pure. . . feeling.

LIZ: Makes me want to go home and clean up my kitchen.

MARGE: Fine, that's fine if that's what it does. But don't you see, the outrage, the striking out for freedom. It's a clarion call for **liberty** for every woman who is tied to three meals a day for the rest of her life.

LIZ: I like cooking.

MARGE: But on your terms, right? Not as a slave to everyone else. That's why I left that Bible study, if you want to know.

LIZ: I was wondering.

MARGE: The Old Testament drives me up a wall.

LIZ: Oh?

MARGE: It has a slavish chauvinistic view of women.

LIZ: You think?

MARGE: I know. Come on, dear. Ruth?

LIZ: The Book of Ruth.

MARGE: The whole thing, from beginning to end. I felt embarrassed for her. I felt myself wanting to apologize to everyone there for what that book seemed to be saying.

LIZ: Ah-hah. So, it has meaning? Content.

MARGE: Words, dear. The difference between words and images. Words have meaning. It's a whole different can of worms.

LIZ: Hmmm.

*(Gesturing towards paintings.)*

What about this one?

MARGE: You tell me. Feeling.

LIZ: Let's see. I feel. . . Let's see. . . red. . . more red. . . lots of red.

MARGE: Good. The red is blood. Old blood. New blood. Blood going on and on. It's the curse you see. All of us women are cursed by blood. It never stops, and when it does, well, then we're over the hill.

LIZ: But blood stands for life.

MARGE: And for death. The blood carries the old eggs away. Down the chute.

LIZ: I'm not sure I want to look at the next painting.

MARGE: Don't you see, God has a thing against women. He has it in for us. He has delimited all of us because of

*(Points to painting.)*

. . . that.

LIZ: So, going back to Ruth. . .

MARGE: Exactly. Here is this woman who loses her husband. So, what does she do? Follows what's her name. . .

LIZ: Naomi.

MARGE: Yeah. I mean when I threw Jack out I swore I would never set eyes on my mother in law again, as long as I lived.

LIZ: You didn't have kids. . .

MARGE: I told him I didn't want kids. He knew that going into the marriage, but the way his mother kept going on and on . . . How could I have had this . . .

*(She gestures around her.)*

With a bunch of brats running around. You see the sign out front: "No food, no drinks, no children."

LIZ: And Ruth?

MARGE: Women today aren't like that. We're made of stronger stuff. We're independent. Self-sufficient. We call the shots. Ruth was a . . . what, a sycophant. . . a follower.

LIZ: Women back in those days. . .

MARGE: But that doesn't make it right, does it? So, what does she do? She goes through the fields picking up leftovers. Then she waits until – who's the guy again?

LIZ: Boaz.

MARGE: Right. She waits until Boaz is asleep and then she uncovers his feet and lays down. At his feet. This woman has no shame.

LIZ: I don't think it was meant to be a come on.

MARGE: That's what I can't buy. Good looking lady, Guy wakes up in the middle of the night. She's down there at his feet. Threshing floor has that sexy smell of grain and sweat—there was more going on here than the story let's on.

LIZ: I think it had something to do with her asking him to act the part of next of kin for her since she had nobody.

MARGE: So why doesn't she just ask him? She leaves with a whole robe full of grain from that little encounter. The pay off. Sex for a good meal or two. It's worked that way from the beginning of time. He buys you an expensive meal and it's his place or yours. I mean she wasn't a virgin; she knew what was going down.

LIZ: I always thought that was a rather brave thing to do.

MARGE: My question is why we are forced to go through things like that in order to get a guy. Look at these paintings. These are all cries in the dark, made by a woman, articulating centuries of subjugation and outrage to male oppression.

LIZ: Is that the artist over there?

MARGE: No. I don't know who that is. The artist is dead. Committed suicide.

LIZ: Oh. But in the end Ruth. . .

MARGE: Gets her guy. I know. Who needs them? This Boaz character doesn't earn her, he doesn't deserve her, he buys her with a plot of land. She comes along with the vineyards and the wheatfields. She's no more than a . . . a piece of something. Chattel.

LIZ: So, you don't see this as a romance.

MARGE: You know what they say. The only cure to love is getting married. She gets married and you never hear from her again.

LIZ: But it's from her and Boaz' children that the line of David comes, and after that Christ himself.

MARGE: So what?

LIZ: So, she had no rights, she was an outcast, and Boaz redeemed the land and her with it. He gave her a name. He gave her offspring. He stepped in for her and redeemed her.

MARGE: He, he, he. So, what did she do to deserve all this redemption?

LIZ: Not much.

MARGE: There, you, see? You take this book out of the Bible and it wouldn't be noticed. I own this business, I'm making it financially, no kids, totally independent, self-sufficient. I don't need any guy to redeem me. Let me tell you, if I ever get married again both Mr. Lucky and I are going to sign pre-nups out the whazoo.

*(New painting.)*

LIZ: But there's nothing. It's blank. All white.

MARGE: That's the point. No ties. It's all you. Whatever you want to make of it. And it's not white, technically it's gray.

*(Person walks on with appetizer tray.)*

Care for some artichoke dip. It's delish . . .

*(LIZ takes one with a napkin. MARGE moves on.)*

Now over here we have her final three paintings. I know it looks like gray, gray, and grayer, but in truth. . .

*(Music up. MARGE continues to talk but can't be heard. LIZ*

192

*looks at artichoke cracker dip she has, folds it in her napkin, and walks in the other direction.)*

*The End.*

In the following sketch reality is stretched a bit as Paul, learning what this new faith is all about and what the implications of his Damascus experience stand for, encounters a noisy goat.

## SKETCH: PAUL AND THE SCAPEGOAT

*(PAUL a young man in his thirties is pacing about surrounded by parchment documents or scrolls and a hair blanket or stole thrown over the back of a chair. A 'goat' comes in, clomping a bit, watches Paul.)*

PAUL: "Surely our griefs He Himself bore, and our sorrows He carried; Yet we ourselves esteemed Him stricken, Smitten of God, and afflicted." Yes, that's it, "he carried our sorrows" Isaiah had it right. And he knew.

*(The GOAT bleats.)*

GOAT: Excuse me.

PAUL: What?

GOAT: Over here.

PAUL: But you're a . . . a goat.

GOAT: That's right. Four hooves, all knees and elbows. And I've been told I smell like a goat too.

PAUL: Yes, I . . . I can tell.

GOAT: Nothing like a wombat. You ever smell a wombat?

PAUL: Not that I know. But you also. . . can converse.

GOAT: I know, you're thinking you've been out here in the wilderness too long, hot sands of Arabia, dehydrated and all, your head stuck in those books all day long, that I'm some sort of apparition. A delusion. But you're looking at the real thing. 100% goat. What's your name?

PAUL: Paul of Tarsus.

GOAT: Uh oh.

PAUL: What's wrong?

GOAT: Tarsus. Heard of that place. Famous for . . . for. . .

PAUL: Making tents and blankets and shirts and togas out of. . . well.
. .

GOAT: Go ahead, say it. Goat's hair.

*(He sniffs blanket.)*

And this, combination of Bezeor and shaggy blacks. Country cousins. Shame.

PAUL: Yes, well, I'm sorry about that. And what brings you here. . . goat?

GOAT: Just passing by when I smelled all that vellum you have sitting around. I was wondering if you might have any scraps laid by. For a late afternoon snack.

PAUL: I'm not so sure. . . I feed you and soon all your friends. . .

GOAT: No problem there. I'm one of a kind. A loner. Not just any goat. I'm a scapegoat. The scapegoat. Ever heard of me?

PAUL: Yes, Leviticus 16:19 (NIV): "Then Aaron shall offer the goat on which the lot for the LORD fell, and make it a sin offering."

GOAT: That's not me. That one got the knife. I'm the other one that gets knocked about. Still one of the chosen, however, and unblemished.

*(GOAT turns around modeling his/her perfection.)*

Whaddya think?

PAUL: Just . . . fine. Aren't you a little far away. . .?

GOAT: From Jerusalem? Been wandering for. . . months. Carrying all these sins that the head priests laid on my head. I tell you, from the weight of things it's been a bad year for the Jews. Those Romans bring out the worst in people. Rebellious spirits, and what I imagine to be the typical load of lust, greed, envy, and appetite. No easy task mine. Especially with all that . . . appetite.

PAUL: But aren't you supposed to die... out there?

GOAT: I suppose. The other goat that was chosen to be God's favorite, he got the knife, — so much for being the favored one. Me? Priest laid on hands, passed over all those sins, cuffed me around the head, and then shoved me out into the wasteland. Been wandering around ever since. But I'm still kickin' as you can see. Haven't died for all these sins yet. Serves 'em right. Speakin' of appetite, you have any leftovers?

PAUL: Uh, nothing that a goat might prefer.

GOAT: You're kiddin' right? Us goats'll eat anything. Like starting right over here. Hmmm. Aged parchment, only the best, and somethin'... ah yes, just the right touch of tannin. You don't mind do you?

   (Picks up parchment scroll to eat.)

PAUL: You can't... spit it out. This is... Deuteronomy. You don't eat it...

GOAT: God's word, right? Supposed to chew on it, right? Digest it, right? What are you doing with all these... words, anyway?

PAUL: This is the Torah, and psalms, and the prophets. I know a lot by heart...

GOAT: So, you wouldn't mind sharing?

PAUL: Not in the way you think. You see, I've met the Messiah, and...

GOAT: The one everyone's been waiting for? Don't see him around?

PAUL: He's revealing the truth to me. He's mentioned over and over in all these... words. And he's showing me how it's him, and how he fulfills all these prophecies, how he...

GOAT: Now wait a minute, who's this... 'he'? This... 'him'?

PAUL: Jeshua, Jesus, the Son of David, the promised one, the... Messiah.

GOAT: So, he just sort of drops in?

PAUL: Not exactly. I read the Scriptures and through the Holy

Spirit he reveals the hidden truths, the connections, how right from Creation all the way through his coming again it's been recorded— all down here.

GOAT: Coming again? You mean he's been, gone, and he's comin' back?

PAUL: That's right. Don't you know? He was crucified and then he was resurrected from the dead.

GOAT: Must have been before my time.

PAUL: Here, listen. . . what I was reciting when you first came in . . .

*(He reads from a scroll.)*

From the book of Isaiah 53:4 (KJV): "Surely our griefs He Himself bore, and our sorrows He carried; Yet we ourselves esteemed Him stricken, Smitten of God, and afflicted."

GOAT: Sounds familiar, sort of what I'm going through. Seems to me you ought to be back in Jerusalem, where all the action is.

PAUL: Well, you see. I haven't always been a follower of Him, of Jeshua, in fact at one time I persecuted his followers. Stood by as they were stoned.

GOAT: Tsk, tsk. Sounds sinful to me. Handful, no, for me it's what I would call a headful of sin. Come, lay your hands up here, as long as I'm alive there might be just a touch of atonement left. Now, I know you're not the high priest, but I think that great shepherd in the sky might still have a little forgiveness left.

PAUL: Uh, goat.

GOAT: Go ahead, don't be bashful.

PAUL: I've got good news and bad news.

GOAT: Start with the good. I've been carrying around all the bad sin stuff for a long time and could use a bit of encouragement.

PAUL: You don't have to be burdened with those sins any longer.

GOAT: I'm listening.

PAUL: The Messiah, the Christ, Jeshua, is our high priest, and not through the blood of goats or calves but through his own blood, he has entered the holy of holies and obtained eternal redemption for all who believe in him.

GOAT: You mean, I'm out of a job?

PAUL: Looks that way.

GOAT: Well, that is a good thing. And now, gulp, for the bad.

PAUL: He's got lots of names.

GOAT: So?

PAUL: And one of them is Lamb of God.

GOAT: Wouldn't you know? Those little woolies always seem to win out in the end. I guess it's back to just chewing on rhubarb in the back forty, but I'm kind of looking forward to that. Chewing. You have a snack or something to keep me going, until then?

PAUL: Well, yes, here. A few pages from Enoch. And a bite or two from the Book of Judith.

GOAT: Can't complain.

PAUL: And maybe just a nibble from Numbers.

GOAT: I'm feeling a bit more. . . lightheaded already.

PAUL: This way.

> (They start off. GOAT starts sniffing a scroll.)
>
> (O.S.)

Goat!!!

GOAT: Comin.' I'm coming.

> (Takes a hoof, slides it over a parchment and licks it.)

Hmmmmm.

> (He exits.) The End.[1]

# Appendix 2

### "Gird Your Minds for Action, Be Sober in Spirit: Christian Ethical Issues in Playwriting" by Sarah Perkins Schulz. (Unpublished essay, Trinity Western University, Canada, 2001).[1]

The age-old debate concerning the relationship of ethical responsibilities to art is no stranger to the theater. Whether from a religious standpoint or not, ethical, or moral dilemmas are often a cause for discussion, especially among Christian theater people—whether actors, directors, or artistic directors—if it seems that something might contradict or compromise their faith. Actors really get into this, debating and taking vastly different stances on such topics as nudity on the stage, use of profane or sexually graphic language, acts of violence, or simulated prayer. This is understandable since they are the ones whose psyches and bodies are inhabiting these actions. Christian producers and artistic directors exercise a certain caution in these areas when they choose which plays to put on, as do the directors themselves in deciding how to stage them.

One group that isn't vocal on the subject are playwrights. These craftsmen are the often-unappreciated backbone of the theater; without them, there would be no (or very few) plays to do. Those who are Christians may offer something even more important: an honest appraisal of faith in an increasingly despairing world. In this position of power, surely ethical issues such as those that concern actors and directors must be dealt with at times. I interviewed seven current Christian playwrights (four men and three women) for this paper, probing their beliefs on several possibly controversial topics, and particularly trying to discover whether they even consider that there are ethical issues that apply to their field. The consensus was strong: yes, there are ethical questions that a playwright must deal with, and though (with one or two exceptions that were unanimously agreed on) my subjects took widely different stances on most of them, it was also agreed that it is important for a playwright to answer and not ignore these questions. They can be divided roughly into three categories: personal responsibility, responsibility to the playwright's theater and audience, and specifically Christian responsibilities.

One topic emphasized repeatedly is that of truth.

Sean Gaffney, playwright and actor, divides this topic in two questions, "Is the play True to itself as story, [and] does it reflect faithfully the reality of the world we live in?" Both were commented on at length, but we'll look at the second one first, since it seems to arouse the most passion. None of those interviewed failed to mention it, and most of them seem to regard this adherence to reality as both an artistic and spiritual necessity for one of their plays. Buzz McLaughlin of the New Jersey Playwrights Center ascribes the power of plays like Arthur Miller's *Death of a Salesman* (1949) to the fact that its "statement [that materialism will destroy you] is true."

"It's important for me to write honest characters, to try to see the virtue in a character who is repulsive to me in some respects and find the repulsive things in a character of virtue, because. . . all of us humans have both. I think this is a playwright's ethical responsibility," says Lucia Frangione, who writes comedy.

The nearly unanimous concern seems to be that the plays take care not to perpetuate a false image of the world or humankind, whether overly negative or overly positive. Ron Reed, playwright and artistic director of Pacific Theater in Vancouver, asserts: "If I write a play about darkness, it's going to be dark . . . because sugar coating evil would be a terrible thought." Along the same lines Gaffney agrees (like Frangione) that "a story that shows a man finding instant solutions to all of life's problems by following the four steps on a religious track wouldn't be True." They both recognize the power of what they are writing, the power of the theater, and that while the greatest good they can do in writing is through being honest about both the wonderful and evil things in our world, the biggest and easiest danger is through giving a voice and face to lies. For a Christian this has additional overtones since it means he or she cannot write religious platitudes. They must work within the boundaries of real human experience—though Gaffney is careful to point out that this does not rule out such imaginative ventures as science fiction. These are wide boundaries, to be sure, but boundaries none the less.

Debra Freeberg adds a note to her affirmation of the need for honesty. "I like to use the phrase speaking the truth in love as a guide—we have the liberty to speak but do we have the license to spew anything out? I don't think so." She is being consciously cautious about how much of the truth and in what way she tells it. A writer of historical plays, Jeanne Murray Walker, presents yet another slant. In her work she often has to create "characters based on real people from the past without much evidence of what they were actually like, so that . . . getting the truth right is always a question . . . [that] becomes more specific if what's being presented is historical."

Not only should plays be true to human reality, but they should also be true to themselves. In short form, this simply means keeping an inner consistency of plot, character, and theme which is a basic recipe for artistic excellence. But for the Christian artist again there is a complication. Should plays be created simply as art forms, or do they need to be justified as teaching tools for instance? This burden is often placed on the artist by disapproving outsiders.

The playwrights interviewed all agreed that plays are simply supposed to tell a story. According to Reed, "[a play] shouldn't be didactic. If you set out to teach, your story won't have room to do what it needs to do." That does not rule out using biblical stories as the basis for a play, as Elvgren, Freeberg, and Frangione have done, but only cautions the purpose they are shaped for. Frangione has real issues with any attempt to "tell a person what to think. Not only is it rude, but it's very ineffectual." Gaffney, on the other hand, has no problem with theater being used as a teaching tool, though he does not feel that is its main purpose: "[It's like] a butter knife [being] used as a screwdriver. And I have used butter knives quite effectively as screwdrivers, so I'm not knocking it."

Just as it is important to preserve the integrity of the story, many but not all playwrights are concerned about preserving their integrity as an artist. The need to put food on the table has plagued many artists, not just theater ones, but the problem is the same: is it ethical to create something that isn't coming from your artistic needs to serve your physical and monetary ones? To sell oneself and one's talents? Ron Reed, Jeanne Murry Walker, and Buzz McLaughlin all refuse to do so. Reed puts his "artistic" view of his work at the opposite end of the spectrum from an "economic" one and cites a reason of faith for his standpoint: "I figure, it's my job to obey God and to follow my heart in these things, and then it's His job to guide the paycheck, one way or another."

But there are those who take economics into consideration. Frangione admits that "economics does effect what I write." She writes comedy that is "suitable for all ages," and tries to make it "refreshing and new" as well as conforming to the limitations of the theater itself (such as a limited number of actors). Gillette Elvgren would be willing to consider "a big film . . . with commercial possibilities. But not if it radically compromised my belief system." Gaffney feels "blessed" because he gets to write both kinds of plays, his own artistic work and commercial projects. He cites the balance as a tricky one, and says, "I fault not the writer who sinks a bit to earn enough money to write their own stuff." But it is clear he regards that as a necessary evil. Telling a story about a friend of his who found a way to be creative within a commissioned work, he comments that her ingenuity let her be "an artist, and not just a prostitute."

There is one limitation all these playwrights observe, one principle that helps ensure that their plays will be staged. They know the theater thoroughly, so they can write around the physical possibilities and impossibilities of a live performance space, including limiting the number of actors to what might fit into a reasonable theater's budget. Jeanne Walker, who often writes on commission, says, "I'm aware of what that theater . . . has . . . does it have a thrust stage, or is it theater in the round? How many characters can you have, how many actors are they going to be able to pay?" The limits of the physical space boost her creativity, rather than strangle it. Frangione also pays attention to some of this but doesn't let it inhibit her storytelling. "I wrote in a camel in *Cariboo Magi*," she says. "Sure, it flickered across my brain that Kevin is going to have a hard time designing a moving camel that we ride, but that's . . . his challenge, and to write it out for fear of the designer not being able to do it, would be an insult to him." Even a self-proclaimed artist like Buzz McLaughlin capitulates to "the market" in this respect. "I realize I can't write plays with big casts, lots of actors, complicated sets because they'll never get done."

For some playwrights, this is as far as they go in contemplating the other artists that make the "profoundly collaborative art" (Walker) that is theater work. Others are very conscious of the actors that they are writing for. Lucia Frangione and Ron Reed were both actors before they became playwrights, and this heavily influences how they write. "I insist on being in my premieres, so I can watch the actors go through the process of bringing the play to life, and I experience it myself," says Frangione. Reed is "an actor first," and he believes that "actors like acting my plays. There's lots of stuff for them because that's where I started, that's my starting place. Kind of the actor's-eye viewpoint . . . in the story." Elvgren, Gaffney, and McLaughlin also take account of the actors, but in different ways. Elvgren changed his degree early in his career to acting and directing, "where [he] learned the economy of writing for the stage . . . from knowing what the actor and the director could do that the playwright doesn't have to." Gaffney thinks of the actors only marginally, attempting to avoid stumbling blocks such as lines that are difficult to speak, or improbable motivations for characters. A common attitude of respect for actors could be summed up in McLaughlin's comment, "I've worked with a lot of good actors, and I know how tremendous they are, so that I can put something in a script and know that a good actor can pull [it] off . . . as difficult as it may seem on the page." McLaughlin does make a point of refusing to exclude potentially controversial materiel out of concern for actors' sensibilities. He "writes for the truth of the character," and believes that everything is fair game for the playwright. Therefore, he refuses to water down his characters' use of foul language just because it might offend someone or give an actor a moral crisis. "If a character comes from a dark, non-spiritual place . . . and uses gritty language, then that actor, Christian or not, should be able to deal with that!" The only limit he has set for himself isn't to use the Lord's name in vain. "It's painful when I hear it . . . so I never have a character say that. And you never miss it, because there's a lot of other ways for people to be upset." Even in that, he limits himself more than some of his colleagues.

The one limit agreed on by everyone is that they cannot, will not, write despairing or nihilistic plays. "Samuel Beckett can write existential drama . . . much better than I can. I don't believe in the subject matter—let him do it," Elvgren says lightly. Frangione adds, "I don't believe that life is all shit and then we die, so I refuse to write like that." She also utterly refuses to write anything that could be seen as propaganda. Gaffney and Walker both believe that limits on what you write are set by your background. "It's a very difficult psychological game . . . to figure out . . . where your limits are," Walker says. Gaffney has tried setting limits—for example, he does not like to write about sexual violation—but they tend not to "hold up in the heat of creation." In that example, there was one play in which a scene of such violation was necessary. Gaffney wrote it. Basically, whatever the story throws at you is "fair game" (McLaughlin). Being a Christian makes little difference in the sense of restricting the scope of the artist. There are some issues that involve only Christian writers, and these include both personal issues of faith, and the more public issue of writing for different audiences: secular or Christian, or both. Some confine themselves to the secular market, like Walker, whose preferred type of play is fitted quite well to such theaters. Reed sees no difference in writing for these two audiences; whoever wants to produce his work is who he's writing for. Another writer who confines himself to the secular market (often) is Buzz McLaughlin, who finds writing for evangelical Christian audiences "much too limiting. [Because] you're preaching to the converted." Frangione and Elvgren both write for evangelical audiences on occasion, and the only difference they see is that here they can count on "a certain shared knowledge in things spiritual" (Elvgren). Frangione takes advantage of this to layer her comedy; a Christian in the audience of her play *Holy Mo* is likely to get a much bigger laugh out of her version of this story because they know that Moses really was an ex-con on the run who got a word from the Lord, though it was from a burning bush in the original story, not a flaming jukebox. But she also likes to fly in the face of the expected, deliberately making the birth of a child in *Cariboo Magi* close to the real thing, blood and screams and all, as possible—after being told that was exactly what her commissioners didn't want. Gaffney seems to be the odd man out on this issue. He actually takes the different sensibilities of a Christian evangelistic audience seriously. On the one hand, this means that he is careful about including offensive materiel such as coarse language and sexual references, saying that it just "guarantees that the audience will stop listening." He also thinks of writing for this audience as a real challenge. "I hate to admit it (being an evangelical myself), but we evangelicals tend to be closer minded when approaching the arts than the general population. If he can catch this audience off guard and suck them into the play, he has really accomplished something." For those who work mostly in the secular market (like McLaughlin) or move between the two (Frangione or Elvgren) there is a unique dynamic that must be overcome. Often their plays are suspect in the secular market since they have been labeled Christian. McLaughlin is sometimes discouraged by this. "It's hard to get through the gatekeepers, meaning the manager and artistic director. A lot of them smell what I'm doing and toss the script out." But he adds that he never knows when he'll find someone even in secular theaters who loves what he's doing. That is probably as rewarding as the encounters he describes with atheists who come up to him after seeing one of his plays and say, "I've been an atheist all my life, but you managed to suck me into the play. I'm upset but you did it" (McLaughlin). But just as often

Christian theater companies reject McLaughlin's work because they do not agree with the way his message is presented, or they are afraid the language he uses will shock their audiences. Elvgren muses about this phenomenon, "[We're] between a rock and a hard place." To get into the secular theaters, McLaughlin says he has to "find stories that contain ideas that I want to deal with that contain spiritual themes . . . and draw them . . . into the story. "

The integration of faith in their plays is almost universally agreed on and taken for granted. As McLaughlin puts it: "Well I can't not do it, 'cause it's my worldview. I mean it's ingrained." Reed claims to have "overt religious content" in most of his plays, but says it is because a playwright must choose "the highest stake issues" he can write about, and for him, most of those involve God. McLaughlin thinks that playwrights should be aware of exactly what they are trying to do with their play and does not believe those who claim that they write without knowing "the themes they are presenting."

The last question in the interview had nothing to do with an actual ethical issue, but rather was one of belief. "Does being a Christian make you different from any other playwrights?" Their responses, while having one element in common, were split basically in two. The majority leaning toward simple humility. "Absolutely," Gaffney says, "being a Christian makes me different from non-Christian playwrights. Just as being American, lower middle class, from a large family, married, and a former tuba player makes me different." Walker gently hints, "I think it could be dangerous to say that I'm so much different from any other playwright . . . I think it might have something to do with pride." Only Ron Reed and Lucia Frangione take it a step further. Frangione: "being a Christian means I can pray; I can commune with that creative energy/Christ/God/inspiration and dance with it and it takes me to places I would have never dreamed of going on my own. This gives me a definite edge." Reed wavers a little more, carefully mentioning the common ground in all the responses—that all artists are endowed with creativity by God. However, to him it seems likely that as a Christian a playwright "spend[s] . . . a lot of . . . time trying to learn to hear the Master's voice and recognize it." So, in a sense, any Christian has a more direct line to the Creator, the source of all human creativity, than a non-believer could possibly have."

According to the results of this research, there are ethical issues associated with the art and act of playwriting They are consciously considered by many Christian playwrights and have a direct bearing on the work these playwrights produce. While playwrights often differ as to the stance that should be taken on some of these issues— which may be in part due to the different types of plays they write—there is also a genuine consensus regarding their mission. Acting as a "prophet to his or her culture" (Elvgren), the Christian playwright is called to present truth, and within that truth, hope for our fallen world that can be found in (or on the road to) God.

Works Cited:

Elvgren, Gillette. Personal interview (email). 10 Dec. 2001

Frangione, Lucia. Personal interview (email). 27 Nov. 2001.

Freeberg, Debra. Personal interview (email). 9 Dec. 2001.

Gaffney, Sean. Personal interview (email). 30 Nov. 2001.

McLaughlin, Buzz. Personal interview (email). 7 Dec. 2001. (1)

Reed, Ron. Personal interview (email). 28 Nov. 2001.

# Appendix 3

## Some Thoughts on Good and Evil
### Gillette Elvgren

When God made us, we alone among all creatures were given the ability — and destiny— to choose between good and evil.

There **is** good; and there **is** evil.

I imagine the problem for the audience and for the writer is when the presentation of either good or evil becomes not black and white, but grey. The conundrum is that we all live in a grey moral universe, we all as fallen creatures, even though we have been redeemed, experience impulses in ourselves that set ourselves up against the standards that God has established.

This is essentially called sin. But we will return to that.

Today's cultural elite basically no longer think of a human being in spiritual terms. What does this mean? It means that insofar as character and morality, self-understanding, repentance, and forgiveness are concerned, there is no moral standard provided for us from God. If not from God, then where do we look? We look to the behavior of the physical universe and evolution for our paradigms of behavior. That means the acceptance of such writers and practitioners as Konrad Lorenz, Darwin, Nietzsche, Freud, and Marx. These are theorists who advocate a human being as a creature who is wholly a product of repressed violent instincts, as well as composed of aggressive territorial tendencies, and of humanistic social contracts. The final product results in a cipher whose behavior is totally determined by aberrant social and environmental influences.

Sin, understood as purposeful separation, denial, and disobedience of God, does not work as a reality in today's culturally elite. Today, a human being is looked upon as a soulless creature whose problems are genetic or environmental.

"Don't worry," we're told, "you're not to blame for your actions, it's not your fault, you can't help yourself. You're just an innocent, an innocent victim."

Sin then, as a conscious rebellion against the living God, is reduced to a clinical psychological vagary. What does this do to the concept of evil? It becomes something that can be explained away or cured through drugs or psychiatric adjustment.

I believe that conscience is the presence of God in us, the friction between the way we are and the way that we could be. The dominant culture would say that conscience is what we're taught by our family, our environment, our form of government so that we can somehow live together. When we understand conscience as having these roots then is it no wonder that one human's sense of sin and acceptable behavior is radically different than another's, and isn't it understandable how we can explain these variables away as being socio- and psycho- logical vagaries that have no lasting repercussions because there are no absolute moral standards?

So let's pull back a bit and look what some choices in film depiction have done since the 1980s. Is Heath Ledger's *Joker* correct in arguing that good and evil are meaningless concepts? Heroes in the last three decades have been co-opting villainous traits (nihilism, sadism, indifference to rules). In comic books "grim and gritty heroes have become all the rage, and that's a shame," says author Neil Gaiman. "Everyone stole all the wrong riffs from *The Dark Knight Returns* and *Watchman*. The idea was to become more ambitious and sophisticated, not more cynical." As heroes became more compromised with negative behavior, and as a green light was given to the villains, they started stealing the show.

So we're somewhat in an era of amorality and the anti-heroic. Issues of character and morality don't play much of a role in films like *Reservoir Dogs* (1992), *Pulp Fiction* (1994), and *Killing Zoe* (1993). There are no heroes in *Pulp Fiction*, so we're forced to identify with the best of a bad bunch.

I believe that we're searching for some sort of a good, and we latch onto anything we can in hopes of finding it. This is a sad situation. But when degrees of evil or aberrant behavior have become the only accepted choice then I believe we as writers and as a culture have lost perspective.

I think if there isn't a true real and meaningful choice by your characters between moral values, or the shadings of such, then your work has lost perspective. The Joker has no choice but to be bad, but Batman struggles with feelings of revenge, justice, and mercy. A character that is addicted has no choice but to act within the limitations of those actions which the addiction dictates. All struggles between the good and evil are lost. A character who is mad is controlled by impulses that are beyond his ability to control physically and mentally. If you believe as I do those moral choices and turning point decisions by your protagonists are important to the development of your story and complement your understanding of how life really works, then to restrict your characters to not being able to make these choices because of addiction or madness is a copout. It's taking the easy way out for both your good guys and your bad guys. If they struggle with addiction and madness, but have some touchstone with moral behavior, then I'm much more open.

To portray evil without the very real possibility of the good working within a situation or a character denudes the entire struggle of both your antagonists and your protagonists. Oh, one can talk of the efficacy of negative transcendence but I've never heard of anyone being led to the acceptance of positive moral values through experiencing nothing but the vapidity of evil, madness, or addiction.

I also think that as believers in the moral ethos prominently put forward by our faith that if we present the dark side in such a way that it is glorified over the light, then we're lying to ourselves, or giving in to impulses that are capable of individual moral corruption.

I also believe that we're playing dangerous games with accepting cultural trends in contemporary storytelling if we purposefully hide our light under a basket. Who are you anyway? What do you believe with all your heart? This doesn't mean that we should shy away from creating stories with difficult and challenging moral issues. Not at all. For example, what does it mean to write with the idea of redemption in mind as a controlling idea? A definition: "the action of saving or being saved from sin, error, or evil." "The improved state of somebody or something saved from apparently irreversible decline." It involves a transformation, hopefully not out of the light into the darkness but the other way around.

Where does the light of your individual transformation shine through in your writing?

# Appendix 4

## Mystery Manifesto

Notes from an informal meeting of Gillette Elvgren, Buzz McLaughlin, and Craig Detweiler at an Arts Within Forum in Atlanta, Georgia (2003).

1. MYSTERY implies tangential worlds, spiritual worlds, other dimensions, time as elliptical—no before and after.

2. MYSTERY implies a sense of destiny. What does it mean to have your name written in the Book of Life? What does it mean to NOT have your name written in the Book of Life?

3. MYSTERY goes beyond the subjective vagaries of the internalization of the mind. For example, in our minds we wander through memory, daydream, projection, and make associational connections that seem to deny that we're grounded in this material reality. But all of this is connected to our psyche and our experiences in material reality. Add MYSTERY to this and you bring in unknowable factors from outside that can be arbitrary; that can't be connected directly with cause and effect; that can be demanding and yet elusive. In other words, mystery isn't a projection of the human mind.

4. MYSTERY is a force and a feeling at the same time.

5. MYSTERY can only be expressed through metaphor, image, contradiction—if you can state it, define it, dissect it, it was not mystery in the first place, and would probably not remain mystery if it was.

6. MYSTERY cannot be proved; it can only be experienced.

7.  MYSTERY has no unities of time, place, and action.

8.  MYSTERY is transfiguration; transcendence; incarnation (the holy indwelling the profane); it is the imbuing of physical reality with transcendental power and meaning.

9.  MYSTERY can be best expressed through the anagogic. (See Flanner O'Connor, c.f., T. S. Eliot, Objective Correlative.)

10. MYSTERY is sought after, it is a journey, but there is no destination in this life. If you stop seeking MYSTERY in this life, part of you dies.

# Appendix 5

## Recommended Plays to Read

Albee, Edward. *Who's Afraid of Virginia Woolf* (1966)

Beckett, Samuel. *Waiting for Godot* (1952)

Brecht, Bertolt. *Mother Courage and Her Children* (1946), *The Caucasian Chalk Circle* (1948)

Chekhov, Anton. *The Cherry Orchard* (1904), *Uncle Vanya* (1898)

Elvgren, Gillette. *Paper Wings* (1995), *Brendan's Journey* (1997), *Steel/City* (1976)

Frangione, Lucia. *Espresso* (2004)

Ibsen, Henrik. *Hedda Gabler* (1891), *The Doll's House* (1879); *Peer Gynt* (1876)

Miller, Arthur. *Death of a Salesman* (1949)

O'Neill, Eugene. *Desire Under the Elms* (1924); *Long Day's Journey Into Night* (1941); *Marco Millions* (1923)

St. Germain, Mark. *Freud's Last Session* (2009)

Shakespeare, William. *Hamlet* (c. 1600), *King Lear* (c. 1606), *Macbeth* (1606), *The Tempest* (c. 1611)

Shaw, George Bernard. *Major Barbara* (1905)

Simon, Neil. *The Odd Couple* (1965)

Sophocles. *Oedipus Rex* (429 BC)

Stoppard, Tom. *Rosencrantz and Guildenstern are Dead* (1966)

Taylor, C. P. *Good* (1982)

Unknown, *Everyman* (c. 1510)

Wilde, Oscar. *The Importance of Being Earnest* (1895)

Wilder, Thornton. *Our Town* (1938), *The Skin of Our Teeth* (1942)

Williams, Tennessee. *A Streetcar Named Desire* (1947), *The Glass Menagerie* (1944)

Wilson, August. *Fences* (1985)

# Glossary

**Act One climax**: A plot point that pushes the protagonist irretrievably into committing to the action of the story problem that is precipitated by the point of attack.

**Act Three climax**: The final and meaningful resolution of the story's plot point progression in which the protagonist now ventures into the final battle and final testing of his will against the forces arrayed against him.

**Act Two climax**: A major plot point that presents the conflict and action late in Act Two in which the protagonist comes closest to relinquishing her objective and being defeated by the antagonist.

**beat**: The smallest motivational building block that is used in structuring the plot of a story in terms of a character's objectives and goals.

**character**: Can be represented through two ways of expressing behavior—

> *characteristics or caricature* represent the surface expression of physical and psychological attributes
>
> *deep character* is how the character is revealed or developed under the demands of action

**character arc**: The formation of what the characters experience in terms of change in physical, emotional, ethical, spiritual, and conscious-awareness states of being.

**context**: Provides the characters with something to physically do on stage that represents their occupation, hobbies, psychological state, and that serve as a secondary avenue for expressing their emotions, wants, and needs.

**crisis moment**: A situation that motivates the central character in a meaningful and usually desperate way toward an inevitable action.

**culture**: A dynamic and ever-changing matrix of the life rituals, habits, philosophies, fads, and passions which are embodied in individual people and in groups or associations of people.

**denouement**: The final section of a play happening after the Act Three climax in which the various threads of the plot are drawn together and relational and thematic matters are resolved.

**differentiation**: The process of bringing different types of characters together in a drama that guarantees variety, conflict, and the potential for different points of view and subplots.

**egocentric representations**: The ways in which characters project their inner thought life, their ego preoccupations, and their subconscious emotional state of mind.

**environmental/contextual representations**: The depiction of the structured worlds in which the characters exist and their effect on the story in terms of what they do (context) in these environments.

**exposition**: Appearing primarily in the openings pages of the playscript as the background information or backstory of the characters, the setting, as well as the presentation of mood that points toward genre creation.

**French scene**: A scene defined in terms of the main characters entering or exiting the stage action.

**happenings**: A performance art form that often breaks the unities of time, place, action, and character in their presentations.

*hamartia*: The Greek word derivate for tragic flaw exhibited by the protagonist in Greek tragedy.

*hubris*: Excessive pride applied as a contributing factor to the protagonist's downfall in Greek tragedy.

**illusory**: Creating the illusions of time, place, action, and character within a dramatic presentation.

**inciting incident/point of attack**: The scene where the action that defines the premise is first realized. It is the beginning of the point of no return for the protagonist, in which he is confronted with a problem and must take action.

**interactive representations**: The important interactions between the main character and family, close friends, lovers, workers, and enemies or antagonists.

**mid-point crisis**: A major plot point occurring just before the intermission break in the middle of Act Two that moves the protagonist closer to (or farther from) their goal.

**monologue (outer and inner)**: a speech that reveals the character's thoughts and emotions, as expressed in two ways—

> *outer monologue* is a somewhat long speech by one character which is usually addressed to another character or characters in the immediate vicinity.

> *inner monologue* is the stream of consciousness that the actor/character creates that is not verbalized but which ensures that the actor is in-the-moment in reacting to what is happening on stage.

**motive**: The truth found in the physical and psychological justification for a character's choices.

**onomatopoeia**: The use or creation of a word that phonetically imitates, resembles, or sounds like the word it describes.

**on the nose dialogue**: Dialogue that states the obvious— information that the audience already knows— or has the characters communicating exactly what they are thinking with little to no subtext.

**plot**: The arrangement of incidents or events in a play that result in a structural cohesiveness in which character, thought, diction, and action come together in a meaningful and unified manner.

**plot points**: The milestone events, reversals, changes, conflicts, and resolutions that provide meaningful shape and direction to the dramatic story.

**premise statement**: A brief paragraph that the writer creates that captures the feeling, flow, and intent of the play idea.

**proscenium stage**: The term for the architectural structure at the front of the stage that frames the action of the play's presentation. It is commonly a rectangular frame, and the stage curtain is directly behind it.

**subplots**: Using subordinate characters who provide varied perspectives on the protagonist(s) problems, and who connect him to different worldviews, provide romantic entanglements, comic relief, and introduce additional progressive complications.

**subtext**: A process of misdirection, saying or doing one thing but meaning another.

**soliloquy (inner driven/outer driven)**: when the character voices her inner thoughts or tells a story without the awareness of someone else being present—

> *inner driven*, in which the audience is not acknowledged

> *outer driven*, where the audience is directly addressed

**street theater**: Composed of simple productions usually by social activist performance artists who choose to stage their work on the street as a means of directly confronting or engaging a public that is non-paying.

**synopsis**: A story outline that is 1–3 pages long, which includes an introduction to the main character, her objectives, the quest she is pursuing, the plot points she creates or encounters, the nature of the antagonist or negative force that opposes her, and a brief coverage of the final conflict and resolution.

**theater**: A live performance presented by people for people that encompasses a series of meaningful dramatic or conflictual events presented in an illusory manner.

**theatrical conventions**: The rules of stage reality established by the playwright that are introduced early in the drama and which often have to do with non-realistic depictions of time, place, and character.

**treatment**: A lengthy document (12–25 pages) which records the action of the play in a scene-by-scene, event by event manner, and is created as a writing aid or guide in composing the play's primary characters, plot points, subplots, all major dramatic conflicts, and themes.

**worldview**: The sum total of our beliefs about the world.

# Notes

## Introduction

[1] Jay Raynor, "Why is Nobody Doing the Right Thing?" *The Observer*, November 11, 2007.

## PART ONE

## Chapter 1
## Story—What It Is and How It Works

[1] Johan Huizinga, *Homo Ludens: A Study of the Play Element in Culture* (Oxford: Routledge, 1949), 6–27.

[2] Flannery O'Connor, "On Her Own Work," in *Mystery and Manners: Occasional Prose*, eds. Sally Fitzgerald and Robert Fitzgerald (New York: Farrar, Straus, and Giroux, 1969), 112.

[3] Bertolt Brecht, "The Street Scene," in *Brecht on Theatre: The Development of an Aesthetic*, ed. and trans. John Willett (New York: Hill and Wang, 1964), 121.

[4] Jean Piaget, *Play, Dreams and Imitation in Childhood* (New York: Norton and Company, 1962), 5–86.

[5] Susanne K. Langer, *Feeling and Form: A Theory of Art* (New York: Charles Scribner's Sons, 1955).

[6] David Steindl-Rast, quoted in *Teaching Science with Stories*, ed. Kevin Strauss, Tales with Tails Storytelling Programs, 2. https://studylib.net/doc/18187632/teaching-science-with-stories.

[7] Friedrich Nietzsche, *The Birth of Tragedy*, from "Quotable Quote," Goodreads, accessed April 4, 2022, https://www.goodreads.com/quotes/7629261-every-culture-that-has-lost-myth-has-lost-by-the.

[8] Robert McKee, *Story: Substance, Structure, Style and the Principles of Screenwriting* (New York: Regan Books, 1997), 213–216.

[9] Bill Harley, "Bill Harley Quotations," Quotetab, https://www.quotetab.com/quotes/by-bill-harley.

[10] Gene Knudsen Hoffman, "Compassionate Listening: An Exploratory

Sourcebook About Conflict Transformation," ed. Dennis Rivers (NewConversations. net, March 2012), 28. https://newconversations.net/pdf/compassionate_listening.pdf.

[11] Michael Torres, *God's Story Structure* (unpublished manuscript, 2021), 18.

## Chapter 2: What Is Theater?

[1] Thornton Wilder, "The Art of Fiction No. 15," interview by Richard Goldstone, *The Paris Review*, no. 15 (Winter 1956).

[2] Michael Kirby, "The New Theatre," *Tulane Drama Review* 10, no. 2, (Winter 1965): 23–43.

[3] Lucia Frangione, *Espresso* (Vancouver, Canada: Talon Press, 2014), 96.

[4] Arthur F. Kinney, "Flannery O'Connor and the Fiction of Grace," *The Massachusetts Review*, 27, no. 1 (Spring 1986): 71–96.

## Chapter 3: The Faith-Based Writer—
## So Where Is the Faith?

[1] Bruce Long, *The Problem with the Dot: A Holistic Approach to Christians' Care and Cultivation of Global Culture through the Theatrical Ecosystem* (Eugene, OR: Wipf and Stock, 2021), 18.

[2] Bruce Long, *Personal Correspondence*, April 2021.

[3] Long, *The Problem with the Dot*, 3.

[4] Sigmund Freud, *Three Essays on the Theory of Sexuality*, trans. James Strachey (New York: Basic Books, 2000), 57.

[5] Long, *Personal Correspondence*.

## Chapter 4: How Then Shall We Write?

[1] H. R. Niebuhr, *Christ and Culture* (New York: Harper and Row, 1975). This book offers different constructs as to how cultures have engaged with Christ in terms of cognizance and applicability. It is a must read for every faith-based artist, who hopefully will be called to become a Transformer of one's culture in terms of Niebuhr's categorizations.

[2] Kenneth Myers, *All God's Children and Blue Suede Shoes: Christians and Popular Culture* (Wheaton, Ill., Crossway Books, 1989), 34.

[3] Henry R. Van Til, *The Calvinistic Concept of Culture* (Philadelphia, PA: The Presbyterian and Reformed Publishing Company, 1972), 32.

[4] Leland Riken, *The Liberated Imagination* (Wheaton, Ill: Harold Shaw Publishers, 1989), 148–149.

[5] Van Til, *The Calvinistic Concept of Culture*, 27.

[6] Marjorie Casebier McCoy, *Frederick Buechner* (San Francisco: Harper and Row, 1988), 108.

[7] Gerald Manley Hopkins, *Gerald Manley Hopkins the Major Works*, ed. Catherine Philips (Oxford: Oxford University Press, 1986), 128.

[8] T. S. Eliot, "Hamlet and His Problems," in *The Sacred Wood* (New York: Alfred A. Knopf, 1921), 92, https://www.bartleby.com/lit-hub/the-sacred-wood/hamlet-and-his-problems.

[9] Flannery O'Connor, "The Nature and Aim of Fiction," in *Mystery and Manners* (New York: Noonday Press, 1969), 82.

## Chapter 5: Inspiration

[1] Zora Neale Hurston, *Dust Tracks on a Road: An Autobiography* (Philadelphia, PA: J. B. Lippincott Company, 1942), 220–221, https://quoteinvestigator.com/2020/08/25/ untold/#f +438270+1+1.

[2] Gillette Elvgren (unpublished poem, 2018).

[3] F. Scott Fitzgerald, "Quotes," BrainyQuote.com, accessed June 10, 2022, https:// www.brainyquote.com/quotes/f_scott_fitzgerald_399449.

[4] Erasmus, "Adagia" (1508), in *Dictionary of Quotations in Communications*, ed. Lilleness McPherson Shilling and Linda Fuller (London: Greenwood Press, 1997), 276.

[5] Francoise Sagan, *The Quotable Quote Book*, ed. Shauna Sorenson (New Jersey: Carol Publishing Group, 1990), 311.

## PART TWO

## Chapter 6: Writing the Play

[1] George Bernard Shaw, *Plays Pleasant: Arms and the Man*, ed. Dan Laurence (London: Penguin Group, 2003), 19.

[2] Gillette Elvgren, *Paper Wings*, in *Faith on Stage*, ed. Dale Savidge (Greenville, SC: Christians in Theater Arts, 2007), 83.

[3] Gillette Elvgren, *Everywoman* (unpublished manuscript produced at Regent University Theater, 2013), 3.

[4] Aristotle, *The Poetics*, trans. S. W Butcher (New York: Dover Publications, 1997), chapters VI–XIX.

[5] Robert McKee, *Story: Substance, Structure, Style and the Principles of Screenwriting* (New York: Regan Books, 1997), Part 3:9, 208–232.

## Chapter 7: The Premise Statement and Story Idea Development

[1] Buzz McLaughlin, *The Playwright's Process* (New York: Backstage Books, 1997), 69–80.

## Chapter 8: Creating Your Characters

[1] Lagos Egri, *The Art of Dramatic Writing: Its Basis in the Creative Interpretation of Human Motives* (New York: Touchstone, 1972).

[2] William Shakespeare, *Hamlet* (New York: Simon & Shuster, 1992) 3.2.

[3] Robert McKee, *Story: Substance, Structure, Style and the Principles of Screenwriting* (New York: Regan Books, 1997), Part 2:5, 100.

[4] William Archer, "The Wild Duck, a Study in Illusions," *The Theatrical World of 1894* (London: Walter Scott, 1895), 136–144.

## Chapter 9: Play Structure and the Beat

[1] Curtis Canfield, personal interview, University of Pittsburgh, 1972.

## Chapter 10: Plot Points and Complication

[1] Tom Stoppard, "The Real Inspector Hound" in *The Real Inspector Hound and After Magritte* (New York: Grove Press, 1969), 11–12.
[2] George Pierce Baker, *Dramatic Technique* (Boston: Houghton Mifflin, 1919), 207.

## Chapter 13: Theme

[1] Georges Polti, *The Thirty-six Dramatic Situations*, trans. Lucille Ray (Manes Knap Reeve, 1924).
[2] Michael Torres, "God's Story Structure" (unpublished manuscript, 2021), 33–34.

## Chapter 14: Dialogue, Monologue, and Subtext

[1] David Mamet, *Glengarry, Glen Ross* (New York: Grove City Press, 1984), 30–31.
[2] Harold Pinter, AZQuotes.com, Wind and Fly LTD, 2022. accessed May 26, 2022, https://www.azquotes.com/quote/425193.
[3] Harold Pinter, *Old Times* (New York: Grove Press, 1971), 7–9.
[4] Gillette Elvgren, *Paper Wings*, 115.
[5] Gillette Elvgren, *Five Cups of Coffee*, Lamb's Players (unpublished manuscript, 2006).

# APPENDICES

## Appendix 1: Writing the Sketch

[1] Gillette Elvgren, "The Ultimate Sketch and Monologue Book," (unpublished manuscript, 1985). All sketches used in this Appendix can be found in this manuscript and were written by Gillette Elvgren.

## Appendix 2: Christian Ethical Issues in Playwriting

[1] Sarah Perkins Schulz, "Gird Your Minds for Action, Be Sober in Spirit: Christian Ethical Issues in Playwriting," (Unpublished essay, Trinity Western University, Dec. 2001).

## Appendix 3: Some Thoughts on Good and Evil

[1] Jeff Jensen, "Batman vs. Joker, Harry Potter vs. Voldemart," *Entertainment Weekly*, March 27, 2009, https://ew.com/article/2009/03/27/heroes-and-villains/.

[2] *Encarta World English Dictionary*, ed. Anne Soukhanov (London: St. Martin's Press, 1999).

# Index